KNOTS YOU NEED

KNACK™

KNOTS YOU NEED

Step-by-Step Instructions for More than 100 of the Best Sailing, Fishing, Climbing, Camping, and Decorative Knots

BUCK TILTON

WITH PHOTOGRAPHS BY BOB HEDE

Guilford, Connecticut

An imprint of The Globe Pequot Press

To buy books in quantity for corporate use
or incentives, call **(800) 962–0973**
or e-mail **premiums@GlobePequot.com.**

Knack is an imprint of The Globe Pequot Press.

Cover photo credits:
Front Cover: © Graeme Dawes /Shutterstock,
© Image Source/CORBIS, © Ken Redding/CORBIS,
© Onne van der Wal/CORBIS
Back Cover: © JackK /Shutterstock

Photos by Bob Hede except where noted.

Text design by Paul Beatrice

Library of Congress Cataloging-in-Publication Data is available on file.

ISBN 978-1-59921-395-8

Printed in China

10 9 8 7 6 5 4 3 2 1

For my wife, Kathleen Hart Tilton, to whom the best knot of all is tied.

Acknowledgments

As thousands of authors have truthfully acknowledged in the past, a book is rarely, if ever, the result of one individual's effort. This author recognizes knotmasters of the past, especially Clifford Ashley and Dr. Harry Asher, and knotmasters of the present, especially Geoffrey Budworth and Peter Owen. He also recognizes the publishing team at The Globe Pequot Press, especially Maureen Graney and Katie Benoit. Thank you all so much.

CONTENTS

INTRODUCTION

Long before mallet and peg, hammer and nail, glue, adhesive tape, or Velcro, there was cordage—and the knots that made it useful. Beside the unknown inventor of the wheel and the forgotten discoverer of fire-making, we should rank equally as a genius the man or woman who figured out how to entangle the ends of vines and plants' fibers in ways that would keep them from untangling.

The tying of the first knot may have occurred more than 100,000 years ago. How else were prehistoric stone ax heads attached to prehistoric axe handles? No evidence, however, remains. But off the coast of Denmark, a fish hook was found still tied to a line (a length of sinew or gut) with what we know today as a clove hitch (see page 36). This hook-and-line was estimated to exceed 10,000 years in age. Part of a knotted fishing net retrieved from a bog in Finland has been dated circa 7200 BC. During the peaks of their civilizations, the Egyptians, Greeks, and Romans tied complex knots for diverse jobs—and left wonders that remain thousands of years later. From the icebound polar regions to the ever-warm equatorial regions, all cultures in all times have knotted cords.

Over the centuries, knots were used by builders, surveyors, soldiers, and sorcerers. The butcher, the miller, the cobbler, the farmer, the weaver, the housewife—they all needed a knot or two, or three. Knots were used for communication, for record-keeping, in religious rites, and for corporal punishment. It was at sea, though, under sail, that the science and art of knot-tying blossomed. As the scope and practice of ships at sea expanded, so did the knots—in both form and function—which made their undertakings possible. Still, it should be remembered, as Geoffrey Budworth writes in *The Illustrated Encyclopedia of Knots:* "For every knot tied aboard ship throughout the last millennium, another was tied ashore."

An exhaustive compendium of knots would be a weighty tome indeed, including today more than 4,000 recognized ways of acceptably entangling cordage. And that number does not include the variations possible with many knots. This book, of course, in no way pretends to be "complete" in the exhaustive sense. It does include 110 knots (yes, one hundred and ten)—more than enough to get every job done. Do you need to know them all? If not, which knots should you know?

The International Guild of Knot Tyers (IGKT), founded in the United Kingdom in 1982, published in June of 1999 from their Surrey branch a list of six knots they think should be known first for use with modern rope. These are the figure 8 knot (see page 22), sheet bend (see page

26), bowline (see page 62), rolling hitch (see page 80), constrictor knot (see page 85), and the round turn and two half hitches (see page 104). They further suggested the figure 8 might be the best overall knot since it can be modified to serve as a stopper, bend, loop, or hitch.

The "Surrey Six," despite its thoughtful creation, may not meet all of your knot needs. An angler may decide the uni-knot is absolutely essential. A decorative knot tyer could declare life impossible without a lanyard knot. A climber may refuse to clip in at mid-rope to anything except the alpine butterfly.

You will need to explore knots, and tie lots, and choose the one or two that consistently meet the demands you place on them. But you are limited only by your willingness to learn. There are many knots fit to be tied.

Today's knots are most often tied by campers, boaters, climbers, anglers, and artisans. This book is divided into those five categories. But knots themselves do not divide neatly. The overhand knot, for example, falls easily into all five categories, as does the double overhand and the half hitch. The bowline is useful in camping, climbing, and boating. And the fisherman's knot is used by campers and climbers as well as anglers.

Despite the overlap, campers will find all the knots they need, and more, in the chapters on camping knots, and the same is true for the other categories. However, I encourage you to read the entire book. As a camper, you may find the knot you have always wanted in the boating or climbing chapter. A boater's soon-to-be favorite knot might be found in the fishing chapter. And the quest for the perfect knot or knots is sure to be, as it always has been, an enjoyable journey.

A bowline.

Knot Terminology

The world of knotting has developed specific meanings for certain words and phrases. The end of the rope or cord used to tie a knot is the *working end,* and the other end is the *standing end.* In between the working and standing ends lies the *standing part*. When a section of cordage is doubled into a U shape, a *bight* is formed, and a bight is the first step in many knots. When a section of cordage is doubled and crosses over itself, it becomes a *loop,* another start for numerous knots. Where the rope or cord crosses itself is known as a *crossing point.* When the working end is not pulled completely through a knot, a *draw loop* is formed, which turns the working end into a quick-release device. A knot that comes undone or untied may also be said to *spill* or *capsize.* To take a wrap around a post or rail is to *take a turn,* but another half a turn around the post or rail creates a *round turn.*

A loop.

A bight.

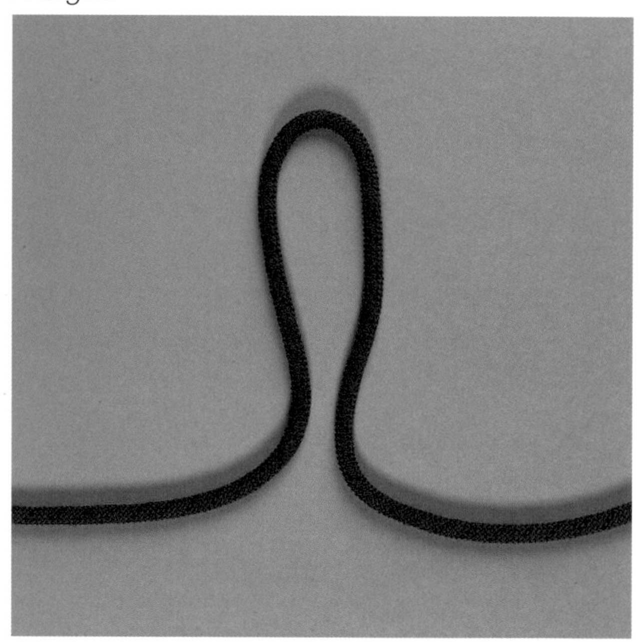

Knot itself can be a generic term applied to any interlacing of flexible material that involves a tucked end or a bight. But *knot* can also have a more specific definition. It can be what ties two ends of the same line together, such as a bowknot in a shoelace, and *knot* typically re-

A draw loop.

fers to anything tied in small stuff such as twine or string. Fishing knots are almost always called knots, regardless of their form or function.

Speaking of function, a *stopper* is tied into the end of a rope to prevent it from slipping through a slit or hole, or to prevent the end of rope from fraying. Stoppers are sometimes tied as simple backups for more complex knots to keep the complex knots from spilling. A *bend* is a knot that joins two separate ropes or cords together. A *hitch* is used to attach a rope to a post, pile, ring, rail, another line, or even to itself.

Knot Nomenclature

Some knots have survived for ages without officially being named, while others are tagged with an unruly list of names. The fisherman's knot, for example, may also be known as the angler's knot, halibut knot, water knot, waterman's knot, English knot, Englishman's knot, or true lover's knot. Additional names for a knot, furthermore, may be unclear. A double fisherman's knot is sometimes called the grinner knot, but the uni-knot is also sometimes called the grinner knot.

A knot's name may also reflect what it looks like. A figure 8 knot looks like its name, and so does a round turn and two half hitches knot. Some knots are named for their inventors: Ashley's stopper, Matthew Walker knots, the Prusik. Some knots are named for their uses: hangman's noose, constrictor knot, cow hitch. And knot names are often misleading. A fisherman's knot is used as a bend; a fisherman's bend is actually a hitch; a midshipman's hitch is really a loop; and a girth hitch is also known as a ring bend. . . . You get the picture. As a final confusing act, occasionally two different knots will bear the same name. The water knot, when referring to the fisherman's knot, isn't the same knot as the water knot when referring to the climbing knot. In the end, the naming of knots is, for the most part, a rather haphazard affair.

Knot Strength

The *breaking strength* of a rope, determined by the manufacturer, tells how much stress or weight that rope will bear before breaking. *Knot strength* refers to how much the knot reduces the breaking strength of a rope compared to the breaking strength of the same rope unknotted. Any rope or cord is strongest when stressed or loaded in a straight line. Any turn reduces strength, and knots turn, twist, nip, and tuck cordage from gentle curves to sharp angles. Therefore, they vary in strength.

The measurement of knot strength, unfortunately, is far from a precise science. It is generally accepted that the overhand knot (see page 18), perhaps the weakest knot, reduces the breaking strength of a rope by more than one half. So the overhand knot is said to be 45 percent efficient, or, in other words, the overhand knot's strength is 45 percent (which means the breaking strength of the rope is reduced by 55 percent).

A turn with the rope doubled.

It should be remembered that a slow and steady pull challenges a rope's breaking strength far less than a sudden shock-load. Only the strongest knots should be used if a rope might be shock-loaded (such as when a climber falls). Also, remember that a knot tied properly is stronger than a knot tied improperly. Or, as the old adage explains: "A not-neat knot need not be knotted."

With relativity in mind, the figure 8 knot (see page 22), the variations on the figure 8, the clove hitch (see page 36), the double bowline (see page 66), and the round turn and two half hitches (see page 104) are considered very strong knots.The girth hitch (see page 98), the double fisherman's knot (see page 108), and the water knot (see page 110). are strong knots. By comparison, a sheepshank knot (see page 88) should *never* be found in ropes of vital importance.

Be not dismayed, however. Modern synthetic ropes and cords are so incredibly strong that they are not often significantly threatened by knots. This book does address knot strength when it seems applicable.

A round turn.

Knot Security

A strong knot, however, is not necessarily a secure knot. Knot security is a different consideration from knot strength. A knot that can be shaken loose to spill of its own accord, such as the bowline (see page 62), is an insecure knot. A knot that slips gradually due to intermittent stresses, such as the clove hitch (see page 36), is an insecure knot. A knot such as the killick hitch (see page 51) may be insecure when pulled in one direction but secure when pulled in the opposite direction. And a knot that holds well in all conditions and in wet, slimy, slippery rope or cord is a secure knot. The vice versa (see page 56) is an example of a secure *and* strong knot. This book addresses knot security when it seems relevant.

Of Ropes and Cordage: Beginning to End

For a knot to exist, something in which to tie the knot must first exist. Traditionally, if that something is over 10 mm in diameter, it is called *rope*. Ropes for special purposes are called *lines*—stern line, tow line, clothesline. Smaller stuff is often referred to as smaller stuff, an informal title, and includes *cord* (which usually refers to large smaller stuff), and then *twine* or *string* (and perhaps *thread*). The smaller stuff is further set apart by its diameter: 5 mm cord, 6 mm cord, and so forth. None of these terms are sacred. Fishing line, for instance, no matter how remarkably thin, is always called *line*, and the word *cordage* may be used to describe both ropes and cords.

The first cordage came from plant and animal fibers. Flax and jute are made from plant stems. Hemp and manila come from plant leaves, and cotton from seeds. Ropes have been created from coconut shell fibers, grass, wool, silk, and hair from horses, camels, and even humans. Excellent cordage has also been made from leather.

Since natural fibers are limited in length to a maximum of about 3 feet, ropes woven from natural fibers are

A stopper knot.

always relatively weak. They also swell when wet, freeze and crack in extreme cold, provide something interesting for insects and rodents to chew on, and require tedious drying before storing. The ends of the fibers stick out from the surface of the cordage, making them rough on the hands of the handlers. All things considered, the development of synthetic fibers was a glorious advance.

Ropes and cordage today are manufactured almost exclusively from nylon, introduced to the domestic market in 1938, and from other more recently developed synthetic fibers. These fibers run continuously along the length of a rope. In addition to being phenomenally stronger and lighter than natural fibers, synthetics handle easier; last longer; and resist abrasion, rot, and mildew. Some of them (polypropylene ropes, for instance) float as well. Being smooth on the surface, they are also easy on the hands. Important on the list of benefits, synthetic fibers stretch when the load is applied, sometimes up to 40 percent, and return to their original length when the load is off. And synthetics can be made in a wide range of colors, from subtle to brilliant. When ropes are arranged close together yet do different jobs, as happens sometimes in climbing, different colors make life easier as well as safer.

Synthetics do have their negative aspects, though. They melt if high heat is applied. Even high friction-generated heat will harden the surface of a synthetic rope, making it less functional. Knots tend to stay tied in "hairy" ropes of natural fibers, but knots tied in synthetics tend to fall apart more often due to the smoothness of the ropes. This has led to the use of backup knots (simpler knots preventing more complex knots from slipping) and the evolution of new knots that are more secure in synthetics.

The making of most synthetic cordage begins with long monofilaments, although sometimes multifilaments (a cluster of very thin fibers) are used. Batches of the filaments are spun together clockwise to make long yarns.

To make a *laid rope* (laid in strands), a batch of the clockwise-spun yarns are spun together counter-clockwise to make a strand. When the required size of strand is reached, three strands are spun together, clockwise again this time, to make the traditional three-stranded rope. It is all the spinning and counter-spinning during the manufacturing process that causes the strands of a rope to cling tightly together.

More often synthetic cordage is braided rather than laid. Most braided ropes are made of two layers, a sheath and a core. The sheath consists of interwoven yarns that protectively enclose the core. The core yarns often run parallel to the length of the rope but may be laid or even plaited (interwoven) if a very large and strong rope is needed. (This sheath-and-core construction is typically called *kernmantle* by climbers.) Occasionally, braided ropes consist of three layers: outer sheath, inner sheath, and core.

A double fisherman's knot.

All cordage, whether laid or braided, may be manufactured with the fibers under high tension and called hard-laid, or made with the fibers under less tension and known as soft-laid. Hard-laid ropes are more durable but also more stiff, especially when new.

A critical aspect of managing rope, no matter what material it is made of, concerns the ends. When the ends are cut, the rope gradually falls apart. Synthetics, lacking the inner cohesiveness of the fibers, fall apart faster than natural fiber ropes. The answer: Do not cut any cordage without first taking steps to prevent unraveling and fraying. There are numerous ways to accomplish this.

Whipping (see page 94) and splicing (see page 90) were once commonly used and still work. *Liquid whipping*, a manufactured product into which rope ends are dipped, is also available. Three-stranded rope ends can be temporarily protected with a constrictor knot (see page 85) tied in twine around the end, or with tape. With synthetic cordage, cutting with a heated knife heat-seals the cut ends. Heat-sealed ends that will see hard use are best backed up with tape or another method of protection against deconstruction.

A bend.

A zeppelin bend.

One thing, by the way, that natural fiber cordage and synthetic fiber cordage have in common is this: High quality products are expensive.

Knot-Tying Tips

Choose the simplest knot that will get the job done. It will be easiest to learn, easiest to remember, quickest to tie, and usually the easiest to untie.

Study and practice in order to tie all knots correctly. Many knots can be tied more than one way. The route seldom matters, but the final configuration is of the utmost importance. A tuck in the wrong direction, for instance, turns a square (reef) knot into an indefensible granny knot.

Knots can be tied right-handed or left-handed, depending on the dominant hand of the tyer. A knot tied right-handed will be the mirror image of the same knot tied left-handed. A few knots have a right-handed element and a left-handed element.

A properly tied knot must be properly tightened. Most

knots must be slowly tightened—shaped, kneaded, molded—into proper configuration, which almost always means there are no gaps in the knot. It is rarely a matter of tugging on the working and standing ends.

Choose the best cordage for the job. A knot works only as well as the rope or cord. Highly elastic cords, such as bungees, shed a bowline (see page 62), but a vice versa (see page 56) holds securely. It is, in other words, not only a matter of the right knot but also the right material to tie it in.

A hitch.

Disclaimers

In order to achieve the maximum photographic effect, the text may refer to one type of cord or line while the photographs show another. The majority of these apparent contradictions occur in the fishing knot chapters, where the knot may be excellent for fine monofilament but it is photographed in heavy fly line. This is because photos of fine monofilament fail to adequately reveal the steps in tying the knots. Trust the text for information, and trust the photo sequences for the proper knot-tying steps.

It is suggested in several places in this book that a specific knot will work, if tied correctly, to save or help save a life. This occurs almost exclusively in the climbing knot chapters. The use of knots in this book to save or help save a life, however, should only be undertaken by people qualified to use the knots appropriately. This is not a how-to book for activities other than the tying of knots themselves.

OVERHAND KNOT

A simple and useful stopper knot that also forms the basis for many intricate knots.

As the most fundamental knot, the overhand stands alone as the knot first learned, often by accident, by anyone who handles rope or cordage of any type. A small stopper, it may not meet the demands of all situations. The overhand is repeated time and time again as part of other knots.

RED ● LIGHT

This knot reduces the strength of a rope by as much as 55 percent. Remove unwanted overhands from mid-rope as soon as possible.

Overhand Knot: Step 1

Create a loop in the working end of a rope or cord.

GREEN ● LIGHT

The overhand is useful in boating, climbing, fishing, and craftwork.

Overhand Knot: Step 2

Take the working end over the standing part and back up through the loop. Tighten the knot by pulling simultaneously on the working end and the standing end.

OVERHAND KNOT WITH DRAW LOOP

A variation of the overhand knot that is slightly larger and much easier to untie.

When a basic overhand knot is tightened over a loop, the loop may be drawn out with relative ease by holding the knot and pulling on the working end. This makes the overhand knot with draw loop a better choice than the basic overhand when the knot will be untied soon or often.

Knot with Draw Loop: Step 1

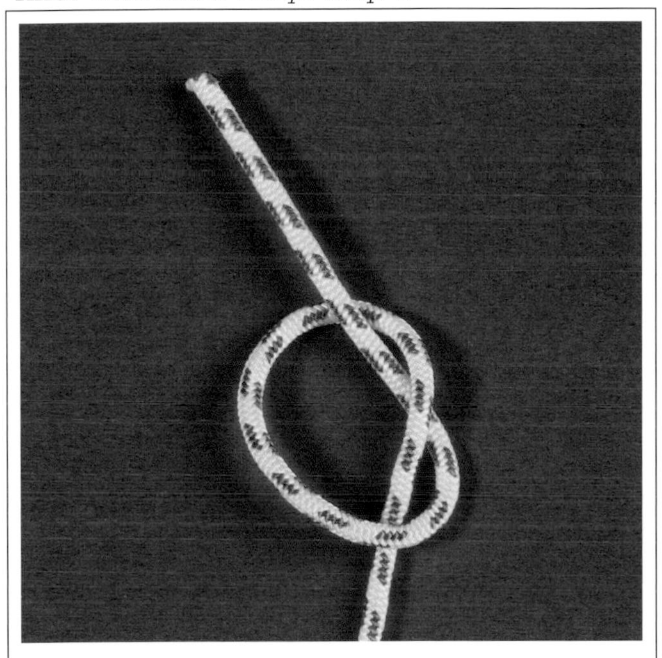

Tie an overhand knot (see page 18) in the working end of a rope or cord.

GREEN LIGHT

This knot is useful in boating, climbing, and fishing.

Knot with Draw Loop: Step 2

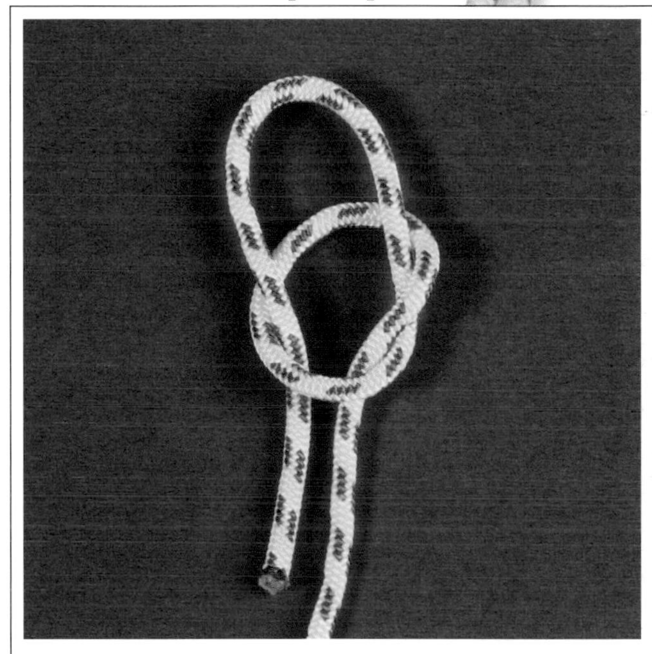

Before tightening the knot, take the working end back through the overhand. Tighten the knot by pulling on the loop and the standing part.

HEAVING LINE KNOT

A large stopper knot that adds considerable weight to the end of a rope.

The weight of the heaving line knot makes it useful for throwing the end of a rope over a greater distance. Tossing the end of a rope intended for hanging a bear bag over the limb of a tree, for instance, is easier with this knot. When a heavy rope needs to be strung across a gap, the heaving line knot can be tied in the end of a lighter line, which in turn is then tied to the heavier line. The lighter line is thrown more easily over the gap, and the heavier line then is drawn (or heaved) behind it. When sailors needed to toss a rope between ship and

Heaving Line Knot: Step 1

Form a loop in the working end of a rope. Bring the working end over the standing part and back under the loop.

Heaving Line Knot: Step 2

Bring the working end back over the loop, compressing the loop.

dock, the heaving line knot worked well. Its other name, the monk's knot, refers to its use by Franciscan monks to weight the ends of the cords they used as belts. In addition to being useful in camping and boating, the heaving line knot is sometimes employed by climbers.

As the turns tighten, form the knot into its final shape.

Heaving Line Knot: Step 3

Make three more turns with the working end around the loop.

Heaving Line Knot: Step 4

After the final turn, bring the working end through the loop, holding the turns around the loop as tight as possible. Tighten the knot by pulling on the working end and the standing part.

FIGURE 8 KNOT

A quick, efficient, and attractive stopper knot.

The figure 8 knot is one of the fundamental knots. However, despite its bulkier appearance, it does not stop a rope from running through a hole or slot any better than a basic overhand. What it does do is untie easier than an overhand, and so it works well when a stopper needs to be tied and untied often. An ancient knot, known since ships first sailed out of sight of shore, its characteristic figure-8 shape also signifies faithful love in heraldry, showing up in numerous coats of arms where it has been given other names, including the Flemish knot and the

Figure 8 Knot: Step 1

Form a loop in the working end of a rope.

This knot is used often in climbing and boating.

Figure 8 Knot: Step 2

Twist the end of the loop to form a second loop.

Savoy knot. The figure 8 forms the basis for many other knots and is, therefore, a knot one needs to know. It can be modified to serve as a bend, loop, or hitch, and it has been dubbed by the International Guild of Knot Tyers as *the* best overall knot.

Notice the characteristic figure 8 shape that gives this knot its name.

Figure 8 Knot: Step 3

Bring the working end of the rope up through the second loop.

Figure 8 Knot: Step 4

Tighten the knot by pulling on both the working end and the standing part.

FIGURE 8 KNOT WITH DRAW LOOP

A variation of the figure 8 knot that is much easier to untie.

When a stopper knot will see only temporary use, the figure 8 with draw loop makes an excellent choice. This knot releases quickly, as any draw loop does, by pulling on the working end. The addition of the draw loop increases the size of the standard figure 8 if a larger stopper is needed.

A favorite in synthetic ropes, figure 8 knots, even this one with a draw loop, may jam in wet ropes of natural fibers. This knot is useful to climbers and boaters as well as campers.

Figure 8 Knot with Draw Loop: Step 1

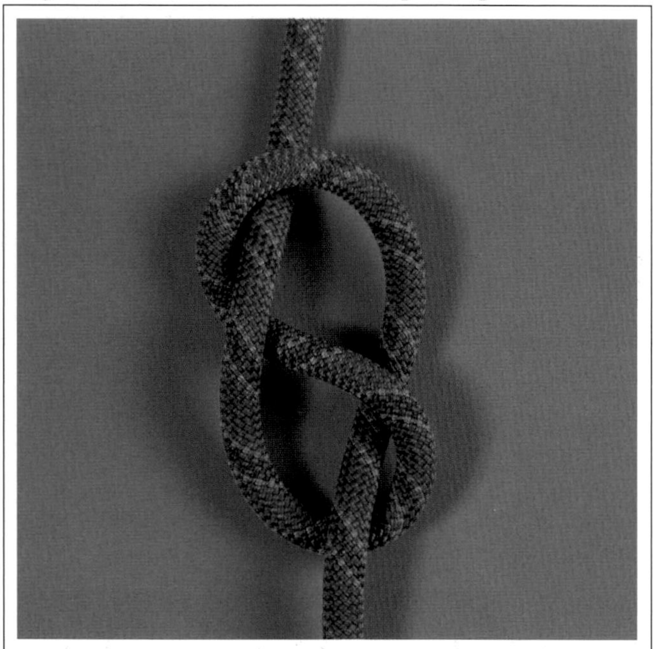

Create a figure 8 knot (see page 22) in the working end of a rope, but do not tighten the knot.

Figure 8 Knot with Draw Loop: Step 2

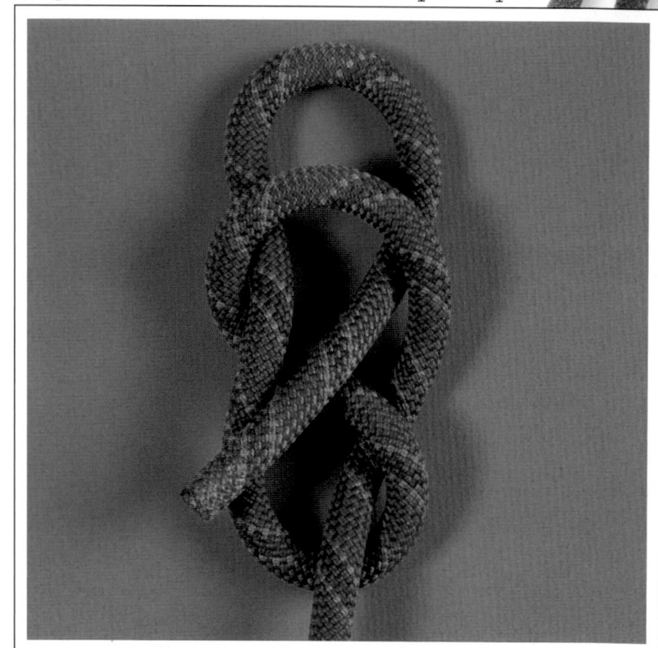

Bring the working end back through the upper loop of the figure 8 but only far enough to form the draw loop. Tighten the knot by pulling on the loop and the standing part.

SQUARE (REEF) KNOT

A quick and simple bend for tying together two ropes or cords of equal diameter.

This fundamental knot, known to many as the square knot, is more accurately called the reef knot. It is used for binding two pieces of cordage of equal diameter or two ends of the same piece of cordage. If improperly tied, as it often is, it becomes the infamous and highly insecure granny knot. Climbers and boaters also use this knot.

RED LIGHT

The square knot loosens easily and should not be used as a bend where security is required.

BENDS

Square Knot: Step 1

Bring the two working ends of the two pieces of cordage together and cross them left over right.

Square Knot: Step 2

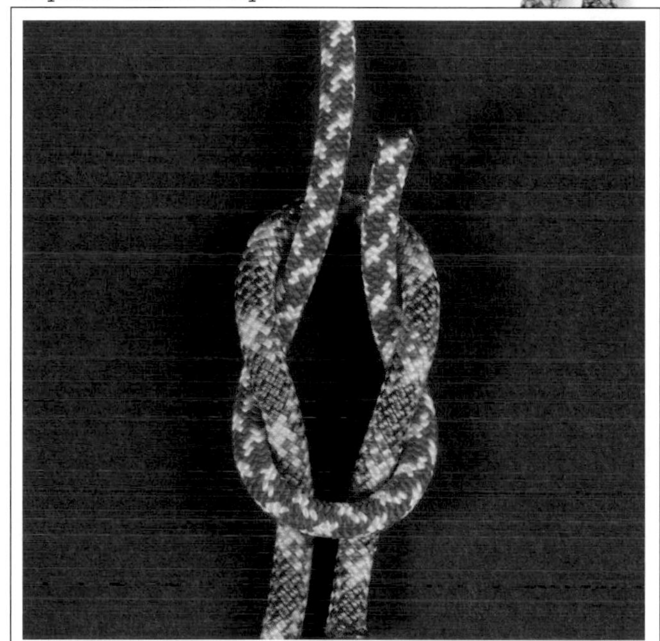

Cross the two working ends a second time, right over left. Tighten by pulling simultaneously on both working ends and both standing parts.

SHEET BEND

A quick and simple bend for tying together two ropes or cords of equal or unequal diameter.

Another fundamental knot and arguably the most commonly used bend, the sheet bend works well in lines of unequal diameter. The strength of this knot, however, decreases in direct proportion to the difference in the diameter of the lines joined. It is more secure if both working ends emerge on the same side of the knot.

If the ropes are unequal in diameter, make the bight in the larger rope.

Sheet Bend: Step 1

Create a bight (see page 10) in the working end of one of the two ropes.

RED LIGHT

Do not use the sheet bend when great strain will be put on the knot because it's not 100 percent secure.

Sheet Bend: Step 2

Bring the working end of the second rope through the bight, then around the back of the bight and across the top of the bight. Then bring it underneath itself and over the other rope, as shown in the photograph. Tighten by pulling on both standing parts.

DOUBLE SHEET BEND

A reinforced version of the sheet bend that provides greater security.

In uses where the basic sheet bend will tend to slip or entirely spill, the double sheet bend creates a more secure knot, even when the ropes are wet and even when the load is heavy. This is especially true when the ropes are of unequal diameter. Due to its greater security, the double sheet bend sees frequent use on boats and ships.

Be sure the turns lie neatly beside each other before tightening.

Double Sheet Bend: Step 1

Tie two ropes together with a sheet bend knot (see page 26).

Double Sheet Bend: Step 2

Bring the working end of the second rope around the bight in the first rope a second time before tucking it under itself, as shown in the final photograph.

FIGURE 8 LOOP

A strong and secure fixed loop for all diameters of material.

The figure 8 loop is one of the most widely known and used loops. Once better known as the Flemish loop, this knot is tied on a bight and, therefore, may also be called the figure 8 on a bight. Since this knot is tied with the rope doubled, the characteristic figure 8 shape is actually a double figure 8, giving the figure 8 loop yet another name: the double figure 8 loop.

Whatever the name, it ties with relative ease and works well in diameters of cordage ranging from fine thread to thick rope. It also ranks high as a secure loop: Once tied,

Figure 8 Loop: Step 1

Create a large bight (see page 10) in the working end and double it over to form a loop.

GREEN LIGHT

This knot is very popular with climbers and also used by boaters.

Figure 8 Loop: Step 2

Bring the doubled working end over the doubled standing part.

it stays tied. Even so, knot experts argue over whether or not the figure 8 loop should be finished with a stopper knot in the working end, a procedure that would eliminate any chance the figure 8 could slip. A stopper can be added with ease if the working end is left long enough. Those who argue against the stopper point out that the figure 8 loop, after being weighted, often proves difficult, but not impossible, to undo.

Figure 8 Loop: Step 3

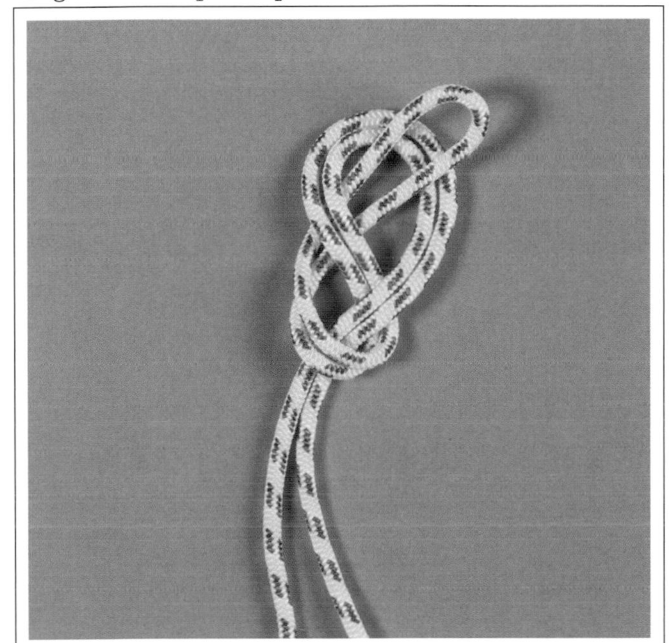

Bring the doubled working end up through the original loop.

Figure 8 Loop: Step 4

Tighten slowly by pulling on the loop and the main standing part to create the characteristic figure 8.

OVERHAND LOOP

A simple and secure fixed loop for use with string or light cord.

Almost as simple as the basic overhand knot (see page 18), the overhand loop creates a quick and useful knot. This knot can be tied in the middle of a rope if a loop is needed there. It also offers another advantage: If a rope has a worn or weak point, the point can be incorporated into the loop, making the rope stronger.

RED LIGHT

This knot can jam when used in rope. Stop jamming by preventing the knot from being too heavily loaded, especially shock-loaded.

Overhand Loop: Step 1

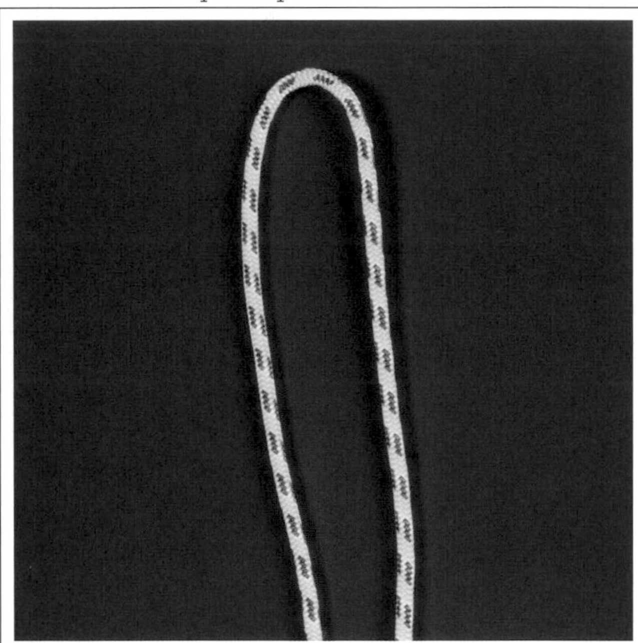

Make a relatively long bight (see page 10) in the working end of the cord.

Overhand Loop: Step 2

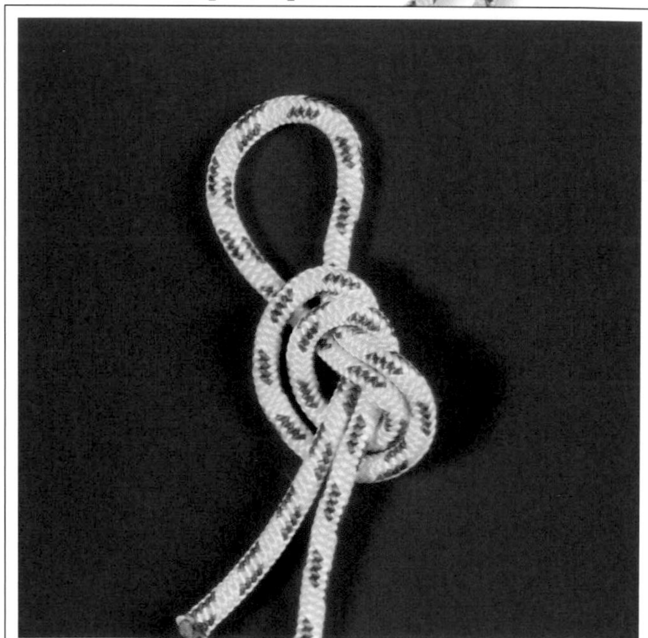

Tie an overhand knot (see page 18) with the doubled cord.

SLIP KNOT (SIMPLE NOOSE)

The simplest of sliding loops that tightens when pulled.

The slip knot, also known as the simple noose, can be tied in any type of cordage material, be it synthetic or natural fiber. It works well as the start of a lashing. This knot appears to be an overhand with a draw loop. However, in an overhand with draw loop, the working end forms the loop. In a slip knot, the standing part forms the loop.

Slip Knot: Step 1

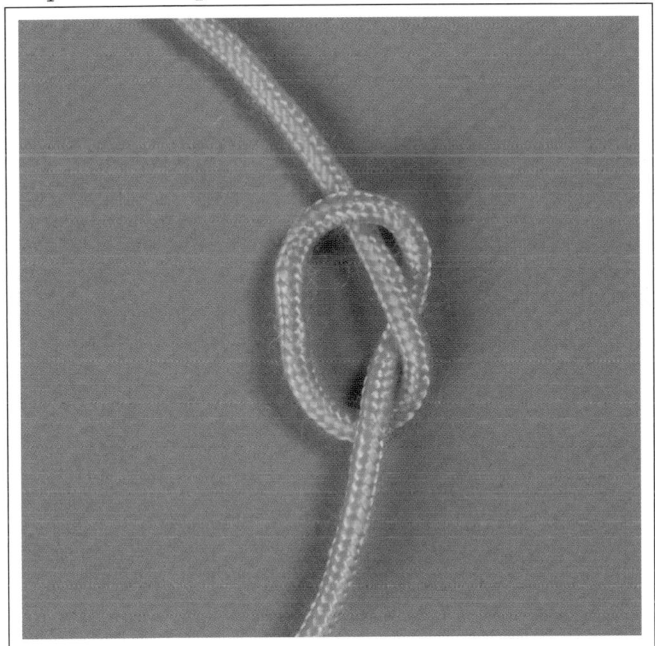

Tie an overhand knot (see page 18) near the working end of a rope or cord.

GREEN LIGHT

This knot may be used in climbing, boating, and fishing.

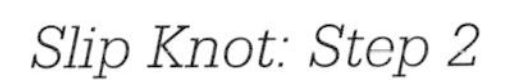

Slip Knot: Step 2

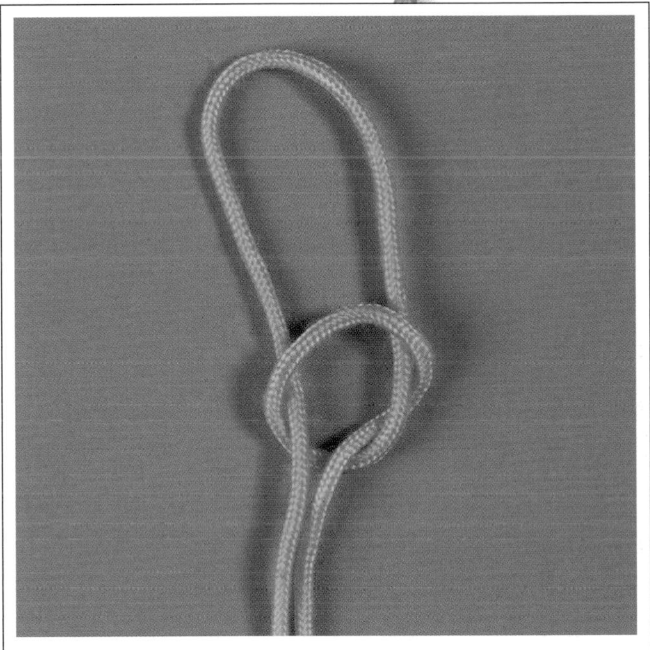

Pull the standing part up, over, and through the loop of the overhand knot. Tighten by pulling simultaneously on the loop created in the standing part and the working end.

HANGMAN'S KNOT (NOOSE)

An extremely strong and secure sliding loop for heavy weights and sudden loads.

The most notorious sliding loop of all time, the hangman's knot, or noose, is able to support very heavy weights and the hard jerk when a large load is suddenly applied. Even with heavy use, the noose unties—but not always with great ease. It does not actually slide with great ease either, and the more turns of the rope around itself during tying, the less easily it slides.

More than 400 years of history in which this knot has seen use suggest that the number of turns should be odd and usually between seven and thirteen, with thirteen

Hangman's Knot: Step 1

Form two bights in the working end of the rope, as shown in the photograph.

Hangman's Knot: Step 2

Bring the working end under both standing parts.

being considered appropriate at an official, court-ordered hanging. Today, as in the past, the loop is typically adjusted to the wanted size prior to weighting the rope.

This knot is sometimes used by anglers to attach heavy swivels to fishing line.

ZOOM

This knot is sometimes used by boaters to secure a thimble (a "hard eye") to the end of a rope without splicing.

Hangman's Knot: Step 3

Begin to make tight turns with the working end around both standing parts, moving from the bottom bight toward the top bight. Make between six and eight turns.

Hangman's Knot: Step 4

Leave enough of the working end to pull it through the last (uppermost) loop. Tighten by pulling on the lower loop.

HALF HITCH

The simplest and most widely used hitch.

Although not very secure, the half hitch quickly fastens a rope to a rail, bar, post, ring, or other object. Despite its name, this is a complete hitch, often used in the working end of a rope to back up and secure another knot that has already been tied. It is seen most often as part of a more complicated knot, but it can be used alone for simple jobs.

RED●LIGHT

The basic half hitch is *not* a load-bearing knot except for simple jobs, such as hanging a food bag out of reach of mice.

Half Hitch: Step 1

Drape the working end over or through the object to which the rope will be fastened.

Half Hitch: Step 2

Bring the working end back out and over the standing part and then through the loop created. Tighten by pulling simultaneously on the working end and standing part.

TWO HALF HITCHES

An advanced variation of the half hitch to create a more secure knot.

Two half hitches bind a rope to an object or another rope with twice the security of a single half hitch. Security is lost, however, if the load is not applied at a right angle to the object. The knot is a half hitch tied on top of a half hitch. It does not have to be constantly loaded, but when it is, the load needs to be constant, or else it will work loose.

Two Half Hitches: Step 1

Fasten a rope to an object with a half hitch (see page 34). Tighten the half hitch.

GREEN LIGHT

This knot is used in climbing, boating, and fishing.

Two Half Hitches: Step 2

Take the working end around again, over the standing part again, and through the loop a second time. Tighten by pulling simultaneously on the working end and the standing part.

CLOVE HITCH

One of the best known and most widely used general hitches.

The simple beauty of the clove hitch, another fundamental knot, and the ability to tie it with one hand, are offset by the fact that it works loose over time, especially if the pull on the rope is not at a right angle to the point of attachment. With that in mind, this knot is still one of the most universally useful of all quick hitches.

Clove Hitch: Step 1

Wrap the working end of the rope around an object, laying it over the standing part as shown in the photograph.

GREEN LIGHT

This knot is used in climbing and boating.

Clove Hitch: Step 2

Wrap the working end around the object a second time and underneath the crossed-over section of the first turn. Tighten by pulling simultaneously on the working end and standing end, taking care to keep the distinctive shape of the knot.

CLOVE HITCH ON A STAKE

A variation of the clove hitch used for tying a rope to a stake.

This method of tying a clove hitch requires two hands but allows the rope to be dropped quickly over a stake or post instead of tying the knot around the object. As a bonus, it can be tied at any point in a rope. An ancient knot, the clove hitch is at least 10,000 years old. When a quick hitch is needed, climbers and boaters use this knot.

Clove Hitch on a Stake: Step 1

Form two loops in a rope, one in the right hand, one in the left, as shown in the photograph.

Clove Hitch on a Stake: Step 2

Place the right-hand loop on top of the left-hand loop. Drop the two loops over a stake and tighten by pulling simultaneously on both ends of the rope, taking care to keep the distinctive shape of the knot.

CLOVE HITCH ON A RING

A variation of the clove hitch used for tying a rope to a ring.

This method of tying a clove hitch to a ring or similar object allows the knot to be easily loosened and retightened to control the length of the rope leading to the ring. It is commonly used by climbers and boaters who need a quick, temporary hitch.

ZOOM

Off the coast of Denmark, under 10 feet of water, this knot was found attaching a prehistoric fish hook to a length of sinew. It was estimated to be 10,000 years old.

Clove Hitch on a Ring: Step 1

Feed the working end of the rope through the ring from behind and bring it down and behind the standing part.

Clove Hitch on a Ring: Step 2

Bring the working end up through the ring again (from the back) and down through the back of the bight of the knot, as shown in the photograph. Tighten by pulling on the standing part.

COW HITCH (SIMPLE)

Another quick and simple, though insecure, general-purpose hitch.

The simple or common cow hitch, scoffed at by knot enthusiasts, loosens easily due to the fact that the weight of a load pulls entirely on the standing part of the rope. It is often used to temporarily tether animals, but it should not be trusted for any length of time.

ZOOM

Archaeological evidence shows that this knot has been around for centuries and deserves a place in knot literature. It will endure, due to its simplicity.

Cow Hitch (Simple): Step 1

Drape the working end of a rope through a ring, as shown in the photograph, or over a rail or bar.

Cow Hitch (Simple): Step 2

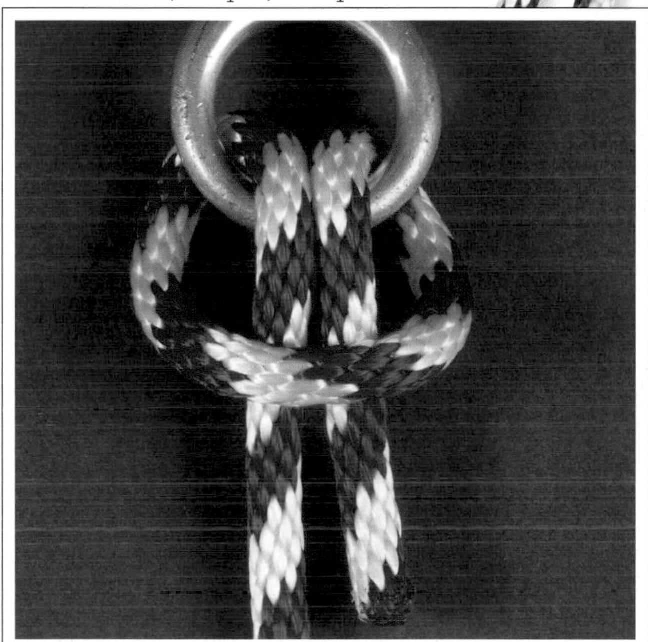

Bring the working end across the front of the standing part, back up and through the ring or over the rail again, and down through the bight of the knot, as shown in the photograph. Tighten by pulling on the standing part.

COW HITCH (PEDIGREE)

A variation of the simple cow hitch that creates a reliable knot.

By tucking the working end of the rope back into the simple cow hitch (see page 39), the pedigree cow hitch is created. That one tuck turns a lightweight and undependable knot into a fairly secure and serviceable knot with numerous uses. And, unlike the simple cow hitch, a load can be applied to the pedigree cow hitch from any angle, making it close to ideal for tethering a cow—or, for that matter, just about any animal.

Cow Hitch (Pedigree): Step 1

Drape the working end of a rope over a rail or bar, as shown in the photograph.

Cow Hitch (Pedigree): Step 2

Bring the working end across the front of the standing part.

It is a handy knot for suspending tools or other items from pegs or cross beams over patios or in garages, sheds, or other storage areas. It also works well as a starting point for lashings. The pedigree cow hitch is credited to Dr. Harry Asher and his 1989 publication, *The Alternative Knot Book*.

ZOOM

Dr. Asher also wrote about the theory behind why knots work He was a founding member of the International Guild of Knot Tyers.

Cow Hitch (Pedigree): Step 3

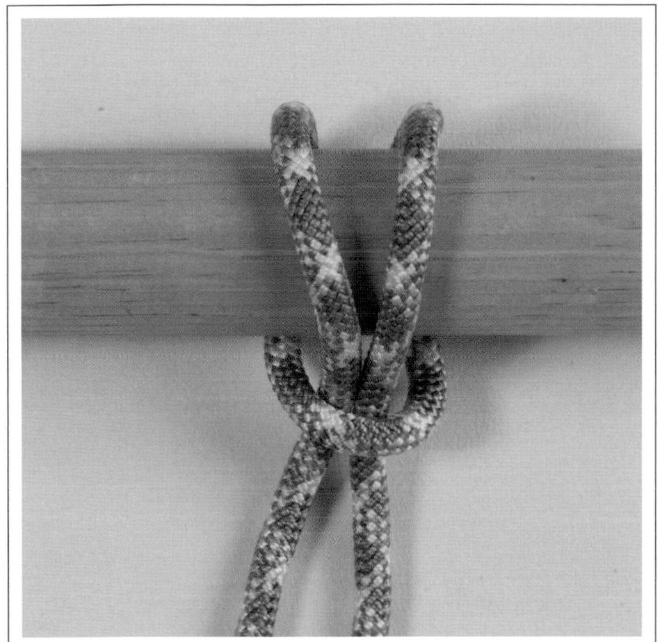

Bring the working end back up and over the rail again, and down through the bight of the knot, as shown in the photograph.

Cow Hitch (Pedigree): Step 4

Tuck the working end behind both turns of the rope that go around the rail or bar. Tighten by pulling on the standing part.

BULL HITCH

An even stronger, "beefier" variation on the cow hitch.

The bull hitch offers stronger security than both the cow hitch (see page 39) and the pedigree cow hitch (see page 40). It is, however, a bit more complex than those knots. Because the bull hitch tends to jam if the standing part is heavily loaded, especially by a sudden jerk, it is most often used as a temporary tether and not in situations where it will be left unguarded for a long time.

Bull Hitch: Step 1

Drape the working end of a rope over a rail or bar and bring it across the front of the standing part.

Bull Hitch: Step 2

Wrap the working end in a complete turn around the standing part of the rope.

ZOOM

A new binding in knot literature, the bull hitch first appeared in print in the January 1995 edition of *Knotting Matters,* the newsletter of the International Guild of Knot Tyers. It is credited to Robert Pont, a member of the International Guild of Knot Tyers.

Bull Hitch: Step 3

Bring the working end up and over the rail or bar (from the back) a second time (as shown in the photograph).

Bull Hitch: Step 4

Take the working end down through the loop in the knot through which the standing part passes. Tighten by pulling on the standing part.

TRANSOM KNOT

A useful knot for tying together two crossed pieces of rigid material.

Back when lashing was more popular in camping, when limbs of trees were freely lopped off and tied together as frames for tents and tarps, the transom knot (called by some the strangle knot) found many uses. It is still a handy knot, useful for securing a pole between two trees from which gear may be hung or to which the high end of a tarp may be attached for shelter.

Survival courses often include this knot as a means to aid in the construction of primitive shelters. It works well in light cord to bind together light pieces of wood, such

Transom Knot: Step 1

With the working end of the rope, make a loop around the vertical piece of rigid material.

Transom Knot: Step 2

Take the working end across the horizontal piece of rigid material and completely around the vertical piece below the horizontal piece, as shown in the photograph.

as when a kite or garden trellis is assembled, and it holds nicely in synthetic or natural fiber cord. It is similar to but slightly less complex than the constrictor knot (see page 85). This knot is typically tied in short pieces of rope or cordage since longer pieces are unwieldy and unnecessary to get the job done.

Transom Knot: Step 3

Cross the horizontal piece a second time. Take the working end underneath itself where it crosses the horizontal piece.

Transom Knot: Step 4

Take the working end underneath the standing part where it forms part of the original loop (as shown in the photograph) and tighten by pulling on both ends of the rope.

TRUCKER'S HITCH

A knot that provides leverage to take up slack in a rope or cord.

The trucker's hitch (sometimes known as the cinch knot or power cinch) is more accurately described as a system of knots giving a three-to-one mechanical advantage that allows tension to be created in a rope or cord. This knot, in other words, works like a pulley, allowing more tension to be created than by simply pulling on the end of the rope. A rope can be drawn as tight as a guitar string, if needed, but the amount of tension is under the control of the knot tyer.

This knot is an excellent method of keeping a tent line

Trucker's Hitch: Step 1

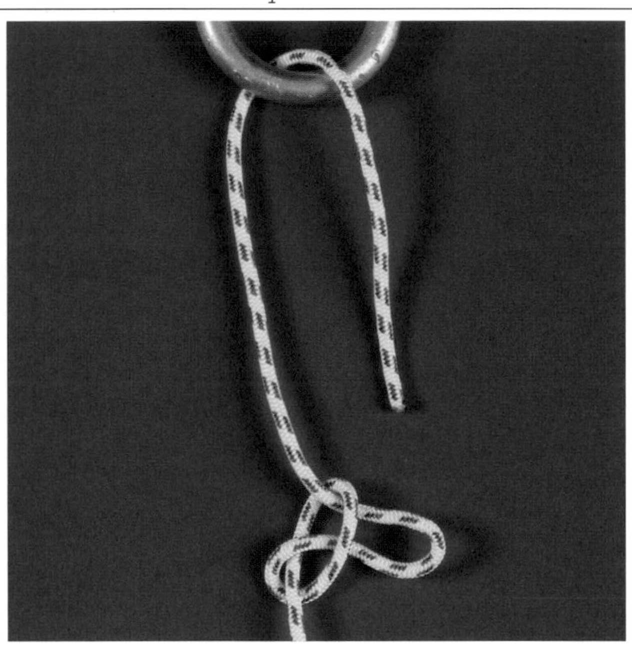

First, tie a quick-release loop, such as an overhand loop (see page 30), an appropriate distance from the working end of the rope or cord. Then pass the working end through the tie-down point (a ring in our photograph, for example).

Trucker's Hitch: Step 2

Bring the working end through the quick-release loop.

GREEN LIGHT

This knot is used in climbing and boating.

taut between the tent and an anchor or for tying a tight line between two trees from which a bear bag can be hung. It also works well for securing gear or a canoe to the top of a vehicle. Once learned, campers tend to wonder how they ever got along without it.

Trucker's Hitch: Step 3

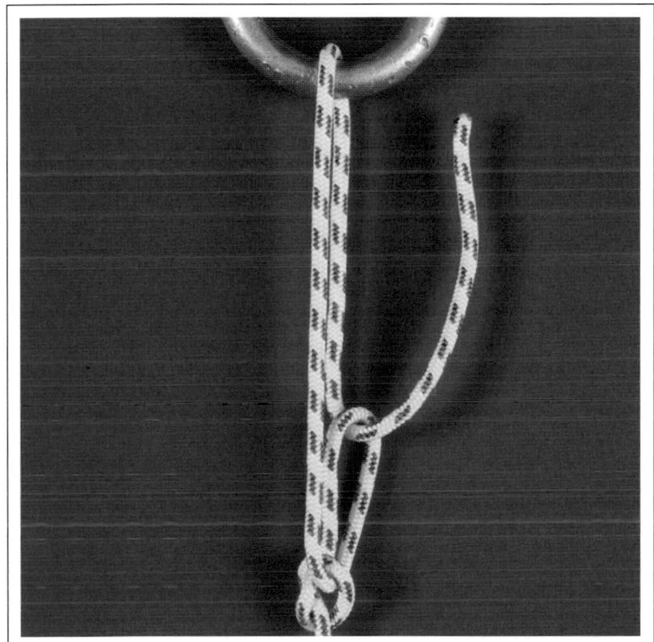

Pull the working end toward the tie-down point to create the amount of tension required.

Trucker's Hitch: Step 4

When appropriate tension is in the rope or cord, secure the knot with a half hitch (see page 34), or an overhand with draw loop (see page 19), as shown in the photograph.

TAUTLINE HITCH

This knot provides leverage to take up slack in a rope or cord.

Like the trucker's hitch (see page 46), the tautline hitch creates a tight (or taut) line but does so with a simple knot instead of a system of knots. Because it is simpler than the trucker's hitch, it is often taught to beginning knot tyers as a method of creating tension, as in a tent line. The knot slides freely but jams against the rope or cord it is tied around when a load is applied. Far more tension can be created with a trucker's hitch, and the

Tautline Hitch: Step 1

Take the working end around or through a secure point and back under the standing part to form a loop.

RED LIGHT

This knot will loosen if slack develops in the rope and, therefore, should be checked often.

Tautline Hitch: Step 2

With the working end, make two or three turns around the standing part within the loop, as shown in the photograph.

trucker's hitch is more secure, so most knot tyers eventually leave the tautline hitch behind. It does find use, however, in securing gear to a rope vertically suspended, such as a rope hanging from the limb of a tree.

ZOOM

Sailors call this knot the rolling hitch; it's useful for attaching ropes to spars (the stout poles that support the rigging). It is far more secure than the clove hitch.

Tautline Hitch: Step 3

Bring the working end down and underneath the standing part outside the loop, as shown in the photograph, forming a second loop.

Tautline Hitch: Step 4

Take the working end through the second loop and tighten by pulling on the standing part. The knot can now be pushed up the standing part, taking slack out of the rope. Under pressure, the knot grips and holds against the standing part, maintaining tension in the rope.

TIMBER HITCH

Temporarily attaches a rope to an object for dragging, raising, or lowering.

A fundamental knot, the timber hitch serves as a short-term noose, quickly tying a rope to a heavy object that needs to be moved by pulling, dragging, lifting, or lowering. It is very secure under tension and never jams. But be careful: Those new to knots often tie this one incorrectly, and then the knot fails.

Timber Hitch: Step 1

Pass the working end around the object to be moved and then behind and around the standing part.

RED LIGHT

Slack in the rope and erratic pulling on the rope can loosen this knot.

Timber Hitch: Step 2

Twist the working end around itself (*not* around the standing part) at least three times. The number of twists can be increased to boost the grip of the knot, depending on the size and weight of the object. Tighten by pulling on the standing part.

KILLICK HITCH

A variation of the timber hitch that provides more security.

When moving a heavy object, especially by dragging or towing (even through water), the killick hitch (a timber hitch with an additional half hitch) creates a more secure bond between rope and object. Sometimes called the kelleg hitch, this knot works well if the object to be moved is long.

ZOOM

Small boats sometimes use this hitch to attach oddly-shaped and heavy objects to the boat as an anchor.

Killick Hitch: Step 1

Tie a timber hitch (see page 50) around the object to be moved.

Killick Hitch: Step 2

At some distance down the rope, add a half hitch around the object, as shown in the photograph.

DOUBLE OVERHAND KNOT

A compact stopper for small- to large-diameter cord or line.

Not only a simple and useful stopper knot, the double overhand works in all sizes of material, from thin thread to thick cord. It shows up as a basis for other knots, including bends, and can be tied in the end of lines to prevent fraying. It is an essential knot to know.

As the knot begins to tighten, twist both ends of the knot in opposite directions with your fingers. Continue to tighten to give the knot its characteristic shape.

Double Overhand Knot: Step 1

Tie an overhand knot (see page 18) in the working end.

GREEN LIGHT

This knot is used in climbing, camping, and craftwork.

Double Overhand Knot: Step 2

Tuck the working end through the loop of the overhand a second time. Tighten by pulling gently on both ends.

ASHLEY'S STOPPER KNOT

A bulky stopper to block holes or slots when smaller stoppers pull free.

When knots that surround the standing part of a line, such as overhands and figure 8 knots, are too small, Ashley's stopper knot does the job. By bringing the working end back into play before the final tightening, a knot of satisfactory bulk is created. Clifford W. Ashley, author of *The Ashley Book of Knots* created this knot.

Ashley's Stopper Knot: Step 1

Tie a slip knot—a simple noose (see page 31)—in the working end.

GREEN LIGHT

This knot is used in climbing and camping.

Ashley's Stopper Knot: Step 2

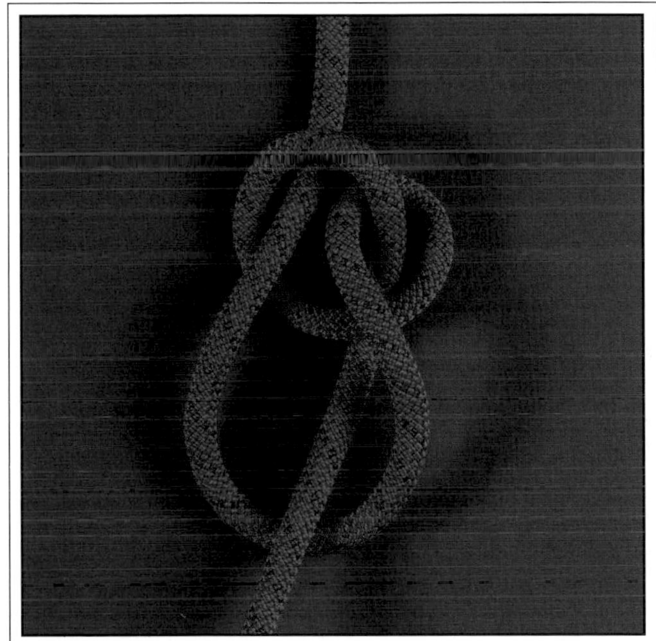

Bring the working end through the back of the noose. For the best results, tighten the overhand before bringing the working end through the loop. Then, tighten the noose by pulling on the standing part to create the three overlapping strands as shown in the photograph.

CARRICK BEND

A knot used for joining two large lines securely.

The carrick bend creates a very stable knot when tied correctly, even when the material in the two lines differs, such as synthetics and natural fibers. But this knot is often tied incorrectly by beginning knot tyers who weave the second working end inappropriately through the first rope's loop. The wrongly tied knot appears, on casual glance, to be a carrick bend, but it falls apart under pressure. Because of this, some knot enthusiasts refer to this knot as the true carrick bend. This knot has been known and often used by mariners for at least one thousand years. It appeared in print for the first time in a book of nautical terms, *Vocabulaire des Termes de Marine*, published in France in 1783.

Carrick Bend: Step 1

Make a loop in the working end of the first line.

RED LIGHT

The carrick bend is mistakenly considered by many a strong knot. It actually reduces the strength of the lines by 30 percent or more.

Carrick Bend: Step 2

Lay the working end of the second line across the first loop, as shown in the photograph.

ZOOM

The carrick bend was chosen as the badge of Hereward of Wake, who led Englishmen in the revolt again William the Conqueror in 1070. It appears in decorative Elizabethan plasterwork adorning Ormonde Castle at Carrick-on-Suir in Ireland, which may explain the name, though experts disagree on the origins of *carrick*.

The working ends on the opposite sides of the knot create a stronger union than when the ends emerge on the same side of the knot.

Carrick Bend: Step 3

Bring the second working end around the back of the standing part of the first line, then over the first working end. Then bring it behind the first loop but over its own standing part where it crosses under the first loop as shown in the photograph.

Carrick Bend: Step 4

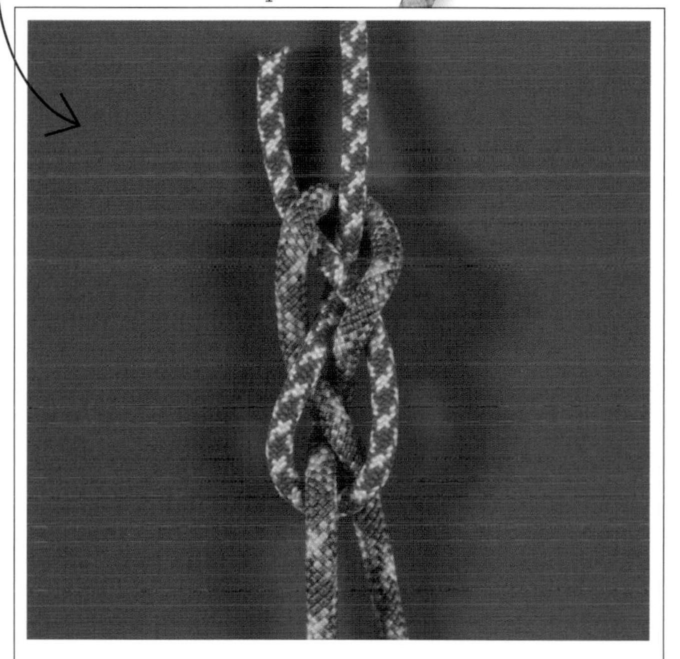

Tighten the knot slowly by pulling on both standing parts. As the knot tightens, it will form the shape shown in the final photograph.

VICE VERSA

A knot used for joining two lines together even when they are wet and slippery.

Slick lines, such as polyethylene or even strips of wet leather, can be joined together firmly with the vice versa. A somewhat intricate knot with quite a few crossing points, it is not terribly difficult to tie. Its first appearance in print seems to be from Harry Asher in *The Alternative Knot Book* (1989), but it, or something very similar, probably saw use by mariners before that. This bend may also be used by climbers.

Vice Versa: Step 1

Lay the two lines alongside each other, the working ends pointing in opposite directions. Loop each line around the other, as shown in the photograph.

Vice Versa: Step 2

Bring the working end of one line through the loop in the other line (from back to front), as shown in the photograph.

RED●LIGHT

If the two working ends are not woven together exactly as shown, the final product will lack the security of a true vice versa and it may utterly fail.

Vice Versa: Step 3

Continue to weave the two lines together by bringing the second working end through the loop in the other line (from back to front), as shown in the photograph.

Vice Versa: Step 4

Work the knot into its distinctive shape as it is tightened, as shown in the photograph.

ZEPPELIN BEND

A secure knot for joining two lines together that can be loaded before it is tightened.

The zeppelin bend (or Rosendahl's knot) can be loaded before the knot is tightened because it will form into its proper shape and function when loaded. This can be a great advantage should a boat being moored drift away before the knot is finished. As with many knots, there is more than one way to tie a zeppelin bend. This method is old and considered by many to be easier. This knot can also be used by campers or by anyone wishing to bend two ropes.

Zeppelin Bend: Step 1

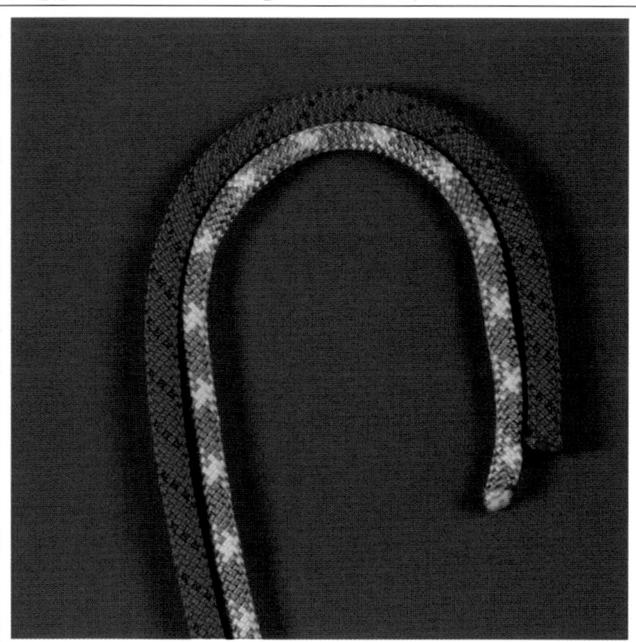

Hold the two working ends alongside each other, both pointing in the same direction, as shown in the photograph.

Zeppelin Bend: Step 2

Tie a half hitch (see page 34) in the nearest line so that it encloses the second line, as shown in the photograph.

ZOOM

This knot was used by the U. S. Navy until 1962 to tether its lighter-than-air ships (zeppelins). Lieutenant Commander Charles Rosendahl, skipper of the zeppelin *Los Angeles* and American aeronautical hero, reportedly allowed only one bend on his airship and on his mooring lines, the zeppelin bend, and thus its other name.

Zeppelin Bend: Step 3

Bring the standing part of the second line away from the first line in the opposite direction and across the second working end, as shown in the photograph.

Zeppelin Bend: Step 4

Bring the working end of the second line through the loop in the first line and through its own loop (as shown in the photograph), forming two interlocked overhands. Tighten the knot slowly by pulling on both standing parts.

SCAFFOLD KNOT

A durable noose (sliding loop) often used with a protective plastic or metal thimble.

More complex than the simple noose (or slip knot), yet simpler than the hangman's noose, the scaffold knot (sometimes called the gallows knot) is a sturdy loop that slides to fit snugly around a bar, rail, or other object. On boats, this knot is often tightened around a thimble, a teardrop-shaped lining for the loop that protects the line from wear, creating what sailors refer to as a "hard eye."

This is important since the almost constant movement

Scaffold Knot: Step 1

Form a loop in the working end of the line, then bring the working end around the back of the standing part.

Scaffold Knot: Step 2

Bring the working end back across the top of the loop.

of boats soon wears through a line. (Thimbles are available in many sizes and materials—such as nylon or stainless steel—and are obtainable from suppliers who sell boating and yachting equipment.) The name suggests that this knot was used by hangmen who were less skilled in knot tying or in a rush to get the job done.

ZOOM

This knot can be used by campers who want a sliding loop more secure than the slip knot. It is often used by fishermen to secure a hook to the end of fishing line.

Scaffold Knot: Step 3

Bring the working end around the back of the standing part a second time, as shown in the photograph.

Scaffold Knot: Step 4

Take the working end up through both loops and tighten by pulling on the working end and the loop. Be sure the turns around the line lay down neatly against each other.

BOWLINE

A fixed loop at the end of a line or for attaching a line to an object.

The bowline is one of the best known and most widely used of all knots. It creates a fixed loop that does not slip or jam. It is, however, far from being a secure knot. It can be shaken loose when unloaded, and it has been known to capsize (deform) when overloaded. It is, therefore, best backed up with a stopper (see the final photograph). But even while loaded, this knot can be untied by pushing up on the bight that surrounds the standing part. When a loop simply has to be untied later, the bowline is a great choice.

Bowline: Step 1

Form a small loop in the standing part of the line and bring the working end back up through the loop, as shown in the photograph.

Bowline: Step 2

Take the working end around behind the standing part and back down through the loop. Pull slowly on the standing part to form the knot.

It is useful in jobs big and small, from securing string before tying a package to securing a gear bag to be hauled up a cliff by climbers. The size of the loop, from very small to very large, is determined by the tyer. More trustworthy variations of the bowline, such as the double bowline (see page 66) and the triple bowline (see page 68), are also covered in this book.

ZOOM

Originally the bowline was used to secure a ship's square sail forward, and closer to the wind. It was mentioned in *The Seaman's Dictionary* of 1644.

Bowline: Step 3

Adjust the main loop to the required size and tighten the knot.

RED LIGHT

The bowline reduces the strength of a line or cord by as much as 40 percent.

Bowline: Step 4

Finish with an overhand stopper (see page 18) to add security to the bowline.

BOWLINE ON A BIGHT

A fixed double loop that can be tied in the middle of a line.

Bowline on a bight, bowline in the bight, bowline upon the bight—they are all names for the same knot. This knot can be tied near a working end of a rope but more often appears away from an end. Historically, this knot served as an improvised seat, the seated person shoving one leg through one loop, the other leg through the other loop. The person in the seat held onto the line and was then lowered or raised, as over the side of a ship. When a double loop is tied in the middle of a rope, a weight (such as a person) can be lowered or raised from two points,

Bowline on a Bight: Step 1

With the line doubled, form a loop in the line as if a basic bowline (see page 62) was being tied.

Bowline on a Bight: Step 2

Take the double end up through the loop, again as if a basic bowline was being tied.

allowing for more security and control during the process. Because devices, such as harnesses, now exist to aid in moving a person via a rope, the bowline on a bight is not recommended for such use except in emergencies. This knot is often used by campers and climbers who need to secure gear to the middle of a rope.

ZOOM

This bowline knot first appeared in print in 1795 in *Allgemeines Wortesbuch der Marine* by Johann Roding.

Bowline on a Bight: Step 3

Open the doubled end into a loop and bring that loop around the double loop.

RED LIGHT

The bowline on a bight reduces the strength of the line by as much as 40 percent. A rope tested to hold 1,000 pounds will theoretically hold only 600 pounds if a bowline is tied in the rope.

Bowline on a Bight: Step 4

Continue to bring the doubled end over the knot that has now been created in the line. Adjust the size of the double loop to the desired dimension before tightening.

DOUBLE BOWLINE

A variation of the basic bowline that adds security to the knot.

A second loop at the beginning of a double bowline doubles the pressure on the working end and provides greater security. The finished knot does not have two loops, even though the name implies that it might. If a double loop is needed, use the bowline on a bight (see page 64).

This knot reduces the strength of a line by only 25 to 30 percent, making it an overall stronger knot than the

Double Bowline: Step 1

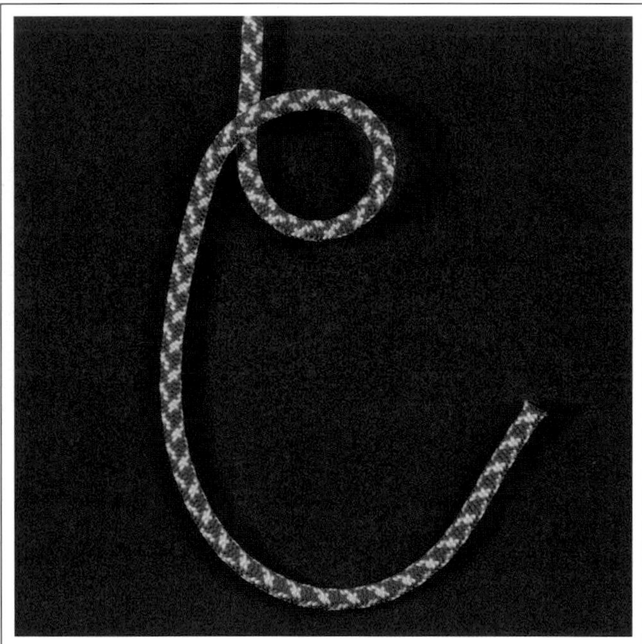

Form a loop in the working end of the rope as if a basic bowline (see page 62) was being tied.

Double Bowline: Step 2

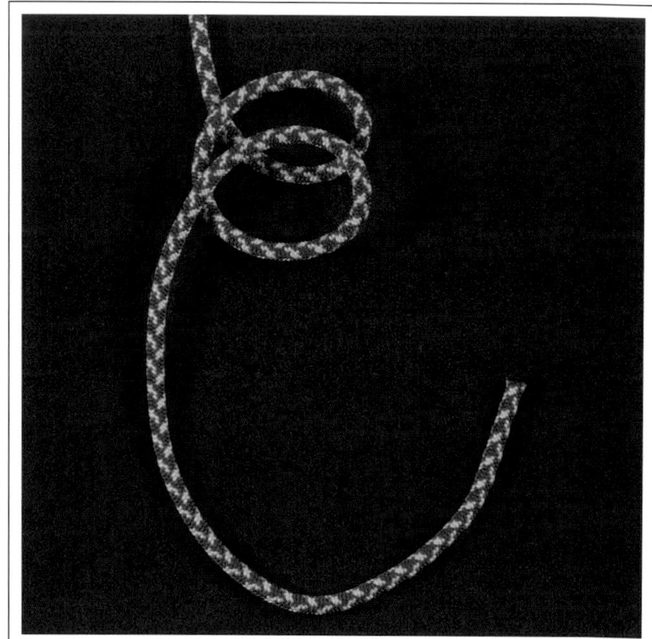

Form a second loop and lay it on top of the first loop.

basic bowline or the bowline on a bight. A stopper knot in the working end also adds security. This knot, as with other variations of the bowline, is often used by campers and climbers.

Double Bowline: Step 3

Bring the working end up through both loops and in back of the standing part as if tying a basic bowline.

Double Bowline: Step 4

Bring the working end down through both loops and tighten the knot. As with the basic bowline, a stopper knot in the working end adds even more security.

TRIPLE BOWLINE

A fixed triple loop at the end of a line, creating a more secure emergency "chair."

The triple bowline is no more than a basic bowline tied on a long bight. Since it is tied on a bight, it can be tied in the middle of a rope. With a fair amount of painstaking effort, the size of each loop can be adjusted to differing sizes. This allows the knot to be used as a chair (with each of two loops around someone's legs and the third loop around the torso under the arms).

As with other knots used as chairs, the triple bowline

Triple Bowline: Step 1

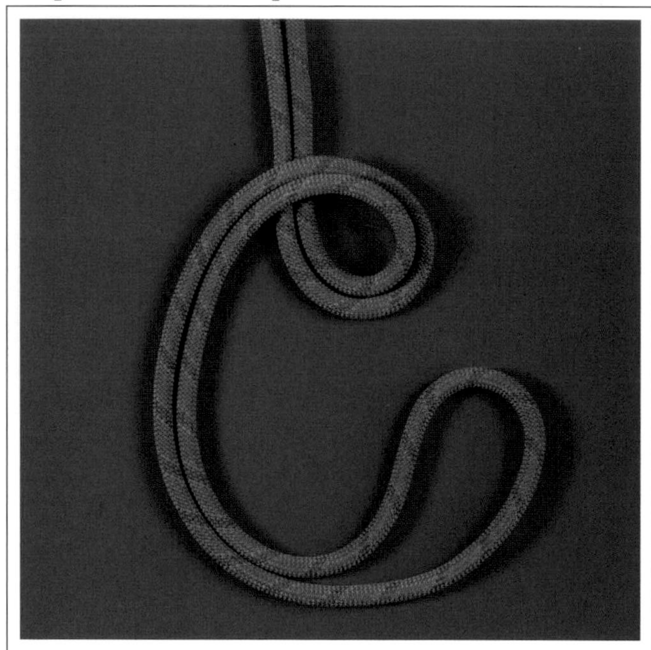

Make a long bight in the working end of the rope and form a loop as if beginning to tie a basic bowline (see page 62).

Triple Bowline: Step 2

Take the doubled end up through the loop and around behind the standing part.

is recommended only when no other means of raising or lowering a person is available. This knot sees very little use today, but it is a classic knot that all skilled knot tyers should know.

Triple Bowline: Step 3

Take the doubled end back down through the loop.

GREEN LIGHT

Although the triple bowline appears in boating knots, it appears to have been developed by climbers to anchor one rope to three different points.

Triple Bowline: Step 4

The doubled end becomes the third of three loops in the finished knot. Adjust the size of the loops and tighten the knot.

RUNNING BOWLINE

A variation of the basic bowline that allows the knot to slide (or run) along the line.

The running bowline is not only strong and secure, but it does not reduce the strength of a line. It slides easily and, as with the basic bowline, unties easily even after heavy use. Tension on the line causes the knot to grip firmly, making the running bowline useful for such duties as hanging or hauling. It is commonly used to toss a loop over something otherwise out of reach, such as an object that has fallen overboard and needs to be retrieved.

Running Bowline: Step 1

Form a bight (see page 10) and a loop in the working end of the rope, and pass the working end under the standing part, as shown in the photograph.

Running Bowline: Step 2

Take the working end around the standing part and down through the loop.

GREEN LIGHT

This knot may be used by campers and climbers who need to haul something along the ground, such as a heavy log, or up the side of a cliff, such as a gear bag. It also works well as the start of a lashing to keep gear on a luggage rack.

Running Bowline: Step 3

Take the working end behind the bight and back through the loop a second time.

Running Bowline: Step 4

Adjust the size of the loop in the line around the standing part and tighten the bowline.

MIDSHIPMAN'S HITCH

A slide-and-grip loop for suspending objects or adding tension to a line.

The midshipman's hitch is another misnamed knot. Not actually a hitch at all, the knot is a slide-and-grip loop that can be adjusted when something needs to be suspended at a specific height or a line needs to have slack taken out. When a load is applied to this knot, it deforms the standing part of the line at enough of an angle to cause the knot to grip firmly. When the load is off, the knot slides freely. If the working end is left long enough, a stopper knot can be tied around the standing part of the line, giving this hitch a semi-permanent position on the line.

Midshipman's Hitch: Step 1

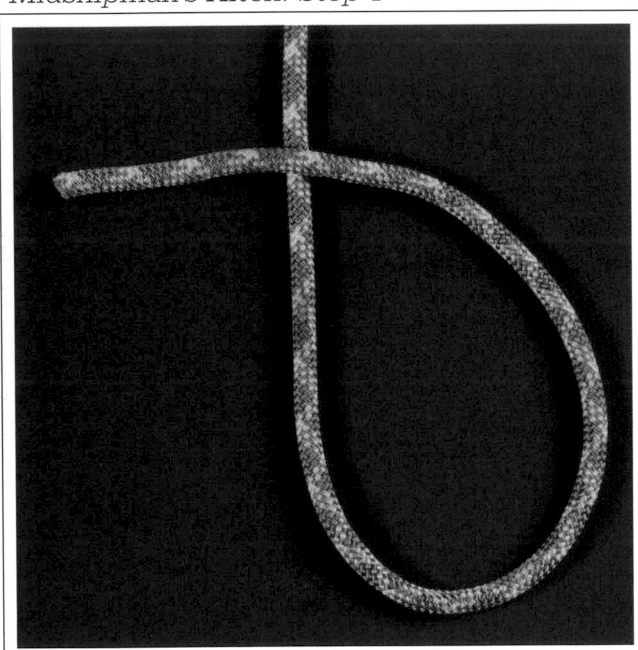

Form a loop in the working end of the rope.

GREEN LIGHT

This knot may be used by campers to add tension to tent lines, by climbers to hang gear, and by artisans.

Midshipman's Hitch: Step 2

Take the working end around the standing part and up through the loop.

ZOOM

There was no officer more junior in the British Royal Navy than one with the rank of midshipman. The name of midshipman's hitch suggests a knot of naval birth that performs less than perfectly. The knot, however, deserves a high rating in utility.

Midshipman's Hitch: Step 3

Take the working end around the standing part and up through the loop a second time, taking care to make the second turn overlap the first turn as shown in the photograph.

Midshipman's Hitch: Step 4

With the working end, tie a half hitch (see page 34) around the standing part above the loop. The knot can be moved to adjust the size of the loop. When it is tightened and the loop loaded, the knot will grip.

ANCHOR (FISHERMAN'S) BEND

A relatively strong and secure hitch, especially for wet or slick lines.

The anchor bend (also known as the fisherman's bend) is another misnamed knot. It is actually a useful hitch, handy for such jobs as securing the mooring lines of small crafts to mooring rings. It's on the strong side, reducing the strength of a line by only 25 to 30 percent, and it works well in lines slippery from wetness or the slickness of the material, such as polypropylene. The anchor bend is a variation of the round turn and two half hitches (see

Anchor (Fisherman's) Bend: Step 1

Take the working end of the line over the anchoring point.

Anchor (Fisherman's) Bend: Step 2

Take the working end around the anchoring point a second time.

page 104). This knot may also be used by campers, to suspend a bag from the limb of a tree, for instance, and by anglers in mooring small fishing boats.

Anchor (Fisherman's) Bend: Step 3

Bring the working end across the standing part and through both turns in the line around the anchoring point.

Anchor (Fisherman's) Bend: Step 4

Snug up the first half hitch and tie a second half hitch around the standing part. Tighten the entire knot.

BUNTLINE HITCH

A very secure knot for conditions where the line and attachment point will be shaken vigorously.

The buntline hitch would be more accurately named a noose since it slides on the line after being tied, but it is used for jobs that require a hitch. It could be described as a clove hitch (see page 36) with the working end tied around the standing part. On sailing ships the buntline was attached to the bottom of sails so they could be drawn up to spill the wind. The hitch, therefore, needed to be secure. This knot tends to jam, so it works in places

Buntline Hitch: Step 1

Take the working end of the rope through or around the attachment point and back across the standing part to form a loop.

RED LIGHT

Do not use this knot when the hitch needs to be untied quickly. When the knot jams, it resists untying.

Buntline Hitch: Step 2

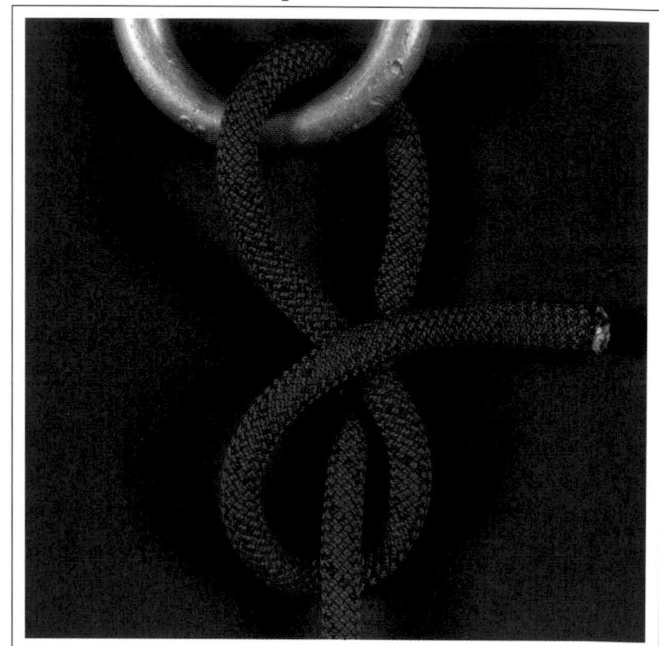

Bring the working end fully around the standing part.

where a strong hitch is needed. This knot may also be used by campers and anglers who need to suspend gear or to tie it down in less than ideal conditions, such as a high wind.

The final tuck of the working end within the knot makes the buntline hitch work.

Buntline Hitch: Step 3

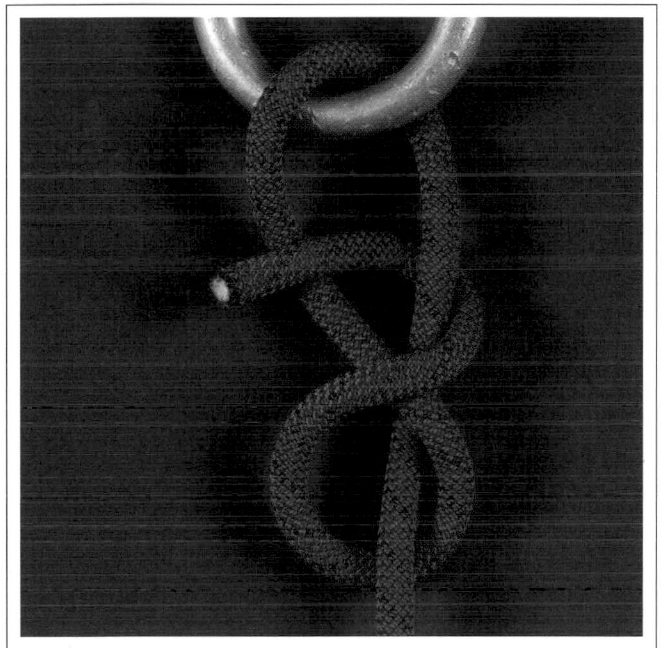

Take the working end around and through the loop from the back, as shown in the photograph.

Buntline Hitch: Step 4

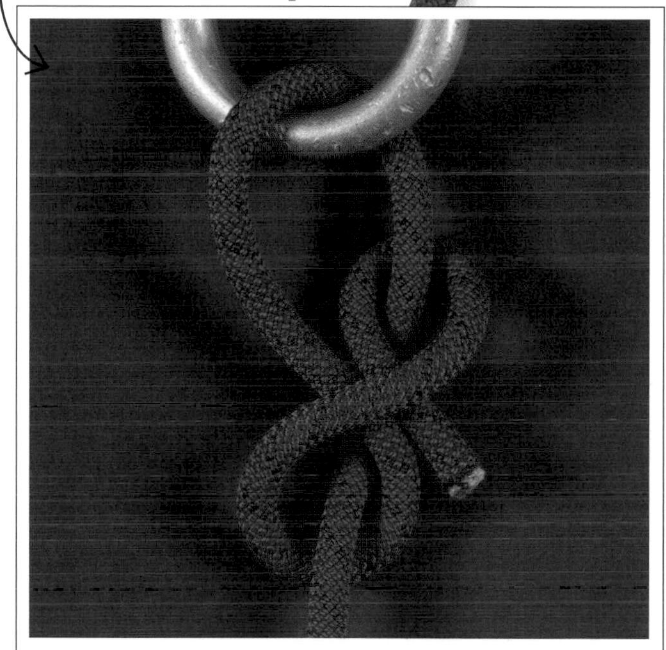

Tuck the working end back through the knot, forming a half hitch. Tighten the knot, then pull the standing part to snug the knot against the attachment point.

HIGHWAYMAN'S HITCH

A knot for situations where a quick release might be needed.

When a temporary hitch is needed, such as mooring a small craft for a short amount of time, the highwayman's hitch (also known as a draw hitch) does an excellent job. It works well for lowering light loads, like lowering a gear bag over the side of a tall ship. Whether or not it was used by highwaymen (robbers) as a quick-release tether for horses, when a fast getaway was a part of job, is not known, but it works well for temporarily tethering animals.

Highwayman's Hitch: Step 1

Form a loop in the working end of the rope behind the attachment point. A long working end will be needed to complete this knot.

RED ● LIGHT

Do not use this knot for heavy work since it can fall apart earlier than required.

Highwayman's Hitch: Step 2

Form a second loop in the working end and pass it over the front of the attachment point.

As a bonus, it can be tied in the middle of a line and released from a distance. This knot may also be used by campers and anglers.

With a quick tug on the working end, the knot falls completely apart.

Highwayman's Hitch: Step 3

Pass the second loop through the first loop.

Highwayman's Hitch: Step 4

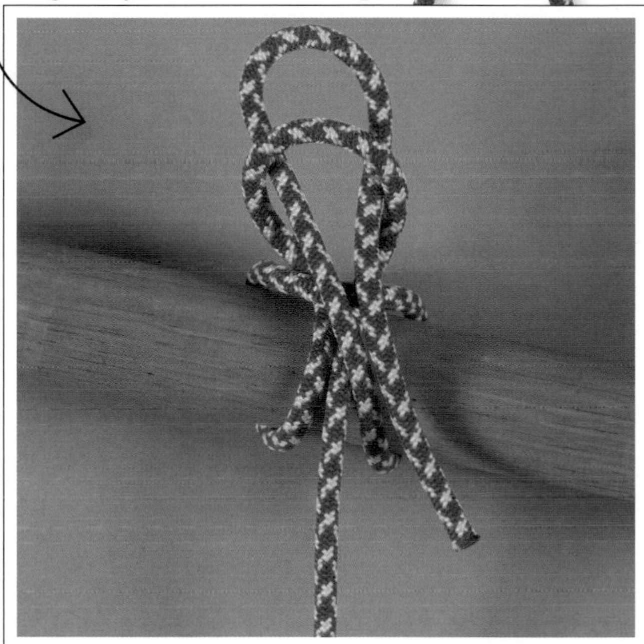

Form a third loop in the working end of the rope and take this in front of the attachment point and through the second loop, leaving enough of a tail on the working end to easily grab. Tighten by holding the third loop in place while pulling on the standing part.

ROLLING HITCH

A knot for situations where the load will be applied at an angle to the knot other than a right angle.

Many hitches suffer a loss of security when the load is applied in a direction other than a right angle. The rolling hitch does not suffer such a loss as long as the tension is relatively steady. It is, in effect, another modification of the clove hitch (see page 36). It works well on any cylindrical object, including the tying of a smaller line to a larger one.

Rolling Hitch: Step 1

With the working end, make two turns around the object or around the larger line.

GREEN LIGHT

This knot is used in camping, climbing, and fishing.

Rolling Hitch: Step 2

When the load is applied, the knot grips the object or line.

Take the working end back up over the standing part. Make another turn around the object or larger line from underneath, and bring the working end out underneath itself (as shown in the photograph). Tighten the turns by pulling on the working end and the standing part simultaneously.

CAMEL HITCH

A knot for situations where the load might be applied in any direction from the knot.

The camel hitch makes an excellent knot choice when the load applied to the hitch might shift from one direction to another. It works well on cylindrical and flat objects, and can be used to attach a smaller line to a larger one. Whether wet or dry, it comes undone easily. And, yes, it would work to tether a camel—or any other animal.

For greater security, make the last two turns into two half hitches (see page 35), one tight against the other.

Camel Hitch: Step 1

With the working end, make two full turns around the bar, rail, or other attachment point.

GREEN LIGHT

This knot is used by campers. One application: attaching a tent line to a stake via a secure hitch.

Camel Hitch: Step 2

Take the working end across the front of the standing part, around the attachment point, and down through itself twice, as shown in the photograph. Work the completed hitch tight by pulling on the working end and standing part simultaneously.

POLE HITCH

This knot gathers and binds together assorted long objects.

Poles, paddles, oars, and any long objects (including long-handled tools such as brooms and rakes) are gathered closely together and bound with the pole hitch. To prevent creating an awkward armload, use two of these knots, one toward each end of the long objects.

The pole hitch not only works for ease of carrying but also for storing long objects. Note that the pole hitch is actually a combination of a hitch with a final securing knot to complete the binding.

Pole Hitch: Step 1

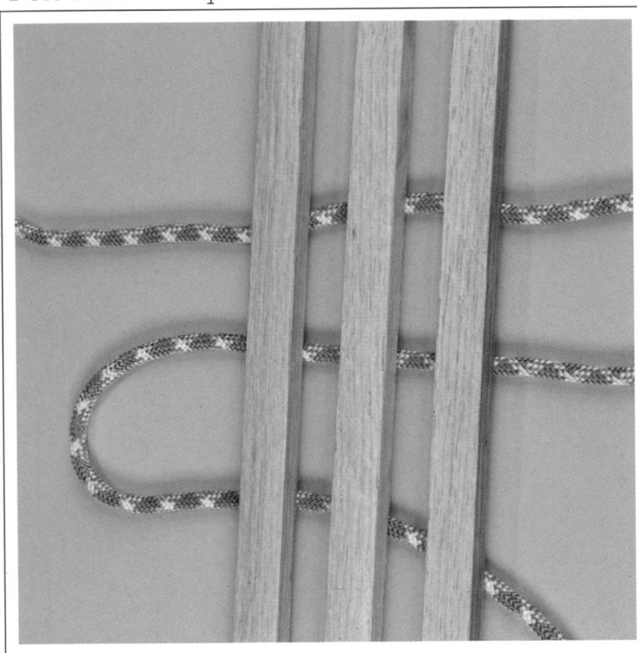

Arrange the cord beneath the long objects in an *S* or *Z* shape.

Pole Hitch: Step 2

Bring the ends of the rope over the objects and through the opposite bights, as shown in the photograph.

ZOOM

When tightening any knot, follow the "work snug and then tighten" guideline. Most knots require some coaxing to tighten. Take out the slack a little at a time, removing it from both the working and the standing ends, until the knot allows no light to pass through its parts. Last of all, give it a tightening tug.

Pole Hitch: Step 3

Draw the objects together, bringing both ends of the rope to the same side of the objects, as shown in the photograph.

Pole Hitch: Step 4

Secure the ends with a square (reef) knot (see page 25).

PILE (POST) HITCH

A quick, simple, and secure attachment to pile, post, or stake.

For fast mooring of a craft to a pile, use the pile hitch. By tying the knot mid-line, tension can be pulled in two directions from the knot, making this great for putting up a barrier rope between a series of uprights. It unties with extreme ease.

Note: The knot can be pushed down the pile or post before being tightened.

Pile (Post) Hitch: Step 1

Double the section of line to be attached and wrap it around the pile or post.

Pile (Post) Hitch: Step 2

Take the loop over the top of the pile or post, then pull on the standing part to tighten.

STORE: 0257 REG: 02/53 TRAN#: 2363
SALE 05/01/2010 EMP: 00349

BORDERS®

Returns

Returns of merchandise purchased from a Borders, Borders Express or Waldenbooks retail store will be permitted only if presented in saleable condition accompanied by the original sales receipt or Borders gift receipt within the time periods specified below. Returns accompanied by the original sales receipt must be made within 30 days of purchase (or within 60 days of purchase for Borders Rewards members) and the purchase price will be refunded in the same form as the original purchase. Returns accompanied by the original Borders gift receipt must be made within 60 days of purchase and the purchase price will be refunded in the form of a return gift card.

Exchanges of opened audio books, music, videos, video games, software and electronics will be permitted subject to the same time periods and receipt requirements as above and can be made for the same item only. Periodicals, newspapers, comic books, food and drink, digital downloads, gift cards, return gift cards, items marked "non-returnable," "final sale" or the like and

CONSTRICTOR KNOT

A binding knot that simply does not come undone.

This variation on the clove hitch (see page 36), once loaded or otherwise fully tightened, refuses to come undone. Fully tightened, it is more often cut off than untied. When used as a semi-permanent binding, the rope or cord can be trimmed off short on both sides of the knot.

Note: When the knot will need to be untied, the final tuck can be made as a draw loop (see page 11).

Constrictor Knot: Step 1

With the working end of the line, tie a clove hitch (see page 36).

GREEN LIGHT

This knot is used in camping, climbing and fishing.

Constrictor Knot: Step 2

Tuck the working end under the first turn of the clove hitch, and tighten.

DOUBLE CONSTRICTOR KNOT

A variation of the constrictor knot that binds even more securely.

When ultimate power in a binding knot is required, the double constrictor, the best of all binding knots, is the answer. It has been compared to the grip of a boa constrictor. When the diameter of whatever this knot is tied to is large, the basic constrictor knot (see page 85) loses some of its strength—and thus the double constrictor would come into play. It can be used, for example, as a substitute for hose clamps.

This knot works extremely well for attaching cords to the handles of tools, or anything else of similar design, to

Double Constrictor Knot: Step 1

Take the working end of the line around the object and across itself.

GREEN LIGHT

This knot is used in camping. One application: as a sack knot to hold closed a gear bag that has no drawstring.

Double Constrictor Knot: Step 2

Take the working end around the object a second time and across itself a second time, maintaining the diagonal direction as shown in the photograph.

allow them to be hung. It can be used to attach a pencil to a clipboard.

The final tuck in tying the double constrictor can be made as a quick-release draw loop if you want to untie the knot later. For the very best results, use a hard rope or cord when tying the knot to soft material, such as a soft line, and use a soft rope or cord when tying the knot to hard material, such a metal ring.

Double Constrictor Knot: Step 3

Bring the working end over the standing part and tuck it under the pair of diagonal turns as shown in the photograph.

Double Constrictor Knot: Step 4

Tuck the working end under the remaining single turn and tighten by working all the slack out of the knot.

SHEEPSHANK

A knot for shortening any line to any required length.

The sheepshank allows a line to be shortened to a required length without cutting. It can also be tied with a damaged section of line in the middle of the knot to take strain off the damaged section. It ties and unties easily and holds well under tension. Two half hitches may be tied at each end instead of one for more security.

A damaged section of line would be in the middle of one of the bights.

Sheepshank: Step 1

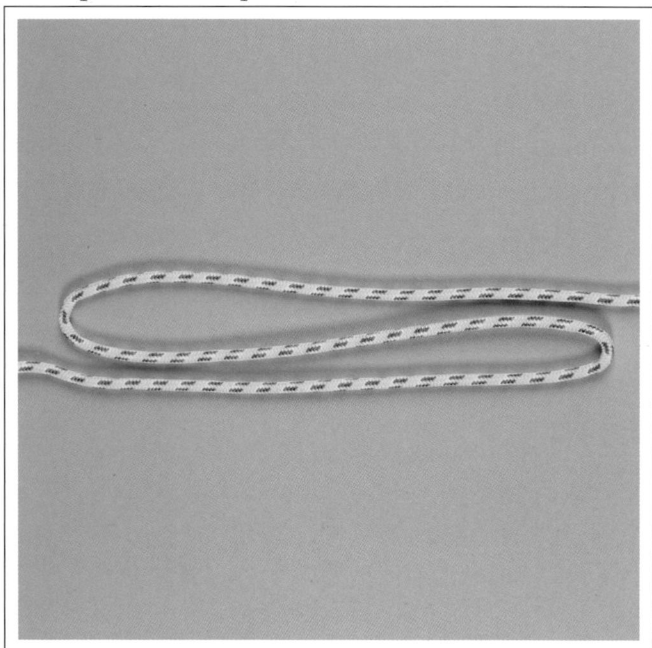

Lay out two bights (see page 10) in the line in an *S* or *Z* shape.

RED ● LIGHT

If the sheepshank is to be loaded, it must be done slowly and cautiously since it can fall apart easily. Fully tighten the knot and apply the load gradually rather than suddenly.

Sheepshank: Step 2

Use the main line to tie two half hitches (see page 35) over the ends of both bights as shown in the photograph. Slowly pull on both the main parts of the line, taking care to keep the knot in its proper shape and form. The two loops at the ends of the knot need to stay approximately the same size.

EYE SPLICE

Used to create an eye at the end of a rope.

For sailors, being able to create an eye, or a loop, at the end of a rope was once considered a basic and important skill. Although ropes with eyes can now be purchased, a reliable one can be made with this knot. This knot can also be useful to campers who need a permanent loop at the end of a rope.

Eye Splice: Step 1

Unlay the end of a rope (separate the strands) and form an eye of the required size. Tuck the end of one loose strand under a strand in the standing part. Tuck the next loose strand under the next strand in the standing part.

Eye Splice: Step 2

Turn the rope over and tuck the third loose strand under the only strand in the standing part that has yet to be used. Repeat the process until each loose strand has been tucked into the standing part three times. Roll the splice between your hands to achieve the proper shape.

BACK SPLICE

A knot that interweaves the strands of a braided rope to prevent fraying.

Traditionally, ropes were made of three strands twisted (or laid) together. When the rope was cut to the required length, splicing was required to prevent fraying. Being able to back splice a rope was considered a basic skill required of all sailors. Some ropes are made with four strands, but this same method of back splicing will work.

Since back splicing serves the same purpose as whipping (tying smaller stuff around a cut end of rope to prevent fraying), this knot is sometimes known as Spanish whipping. Unlike whipping, a back splice actually

Back Splice: Step 1

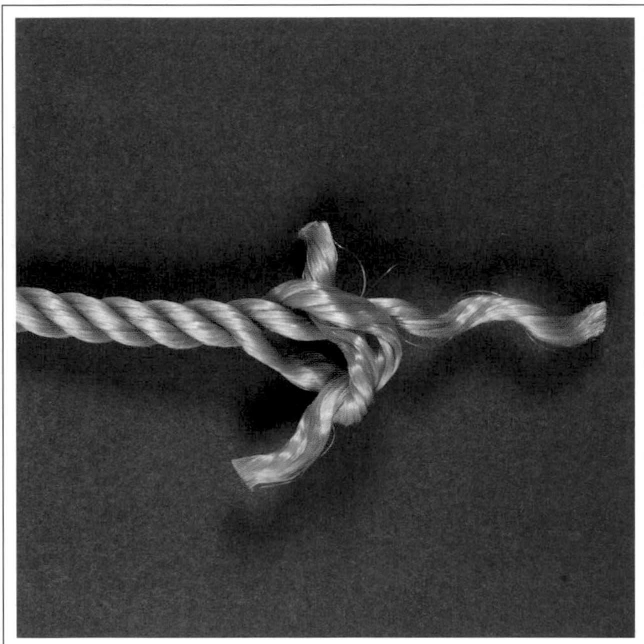

Begin by interweaving the strands into a knot known as a crown, as shown in the photograph. Do this by forming a bight in each strand, then tucking the end of the adjacent strand through the bight. Work clockwise around the unraveled end of the rope.

Back Splice: Step 2

Tighten the crown knot against the end of the rope. Splicing can start now.

becomes stronger with use. It can be used to finish the end of laid ropes used for decorative purposes. A similar interweaving of strands can be used to splice two ropes into one.

Back Splice: Step 3

Lead one strand against the *lay* of the rope (the direction of the twists of the strands). Go over the next strand and under the third strand. Do this with all three stands, making sure the strands leave the crown at regular intervals, each strand centered on approximately one-third of the circumference of the rope.

Back Splice: Step 4

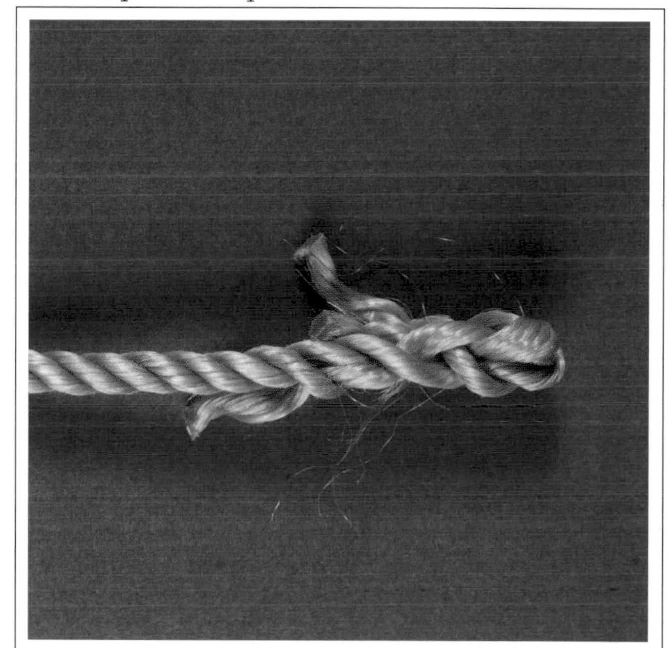

Continue to weave the three stands against the lay of the rope, over and under, until each strand is tucked back into the rope two or three times. The strand ends may be trimmed off, but do not trim them too short since the splice can unravel. Roll the splice between your hands to make it uniformly round.

ASHER'S BOTTLE SLING

Used for hanging a bottle or other similar container of liquid.

On board a ship, bottles of liquid—bottles of water, stove fuel, alcoholic beverages—can slip, slide, fall, spill, or break open. This is one of several sling knots that grip the necks of containers, glass bottle or otherwise, allowing the container to be hung safely aside or carried with greater ease. Asher's bottle sling is credited to Dr. Harry Asher and first appeared in print in *A New System of Knotting, Volume 2,* published in 1989.

Asher's Bottle Sling: Step 1

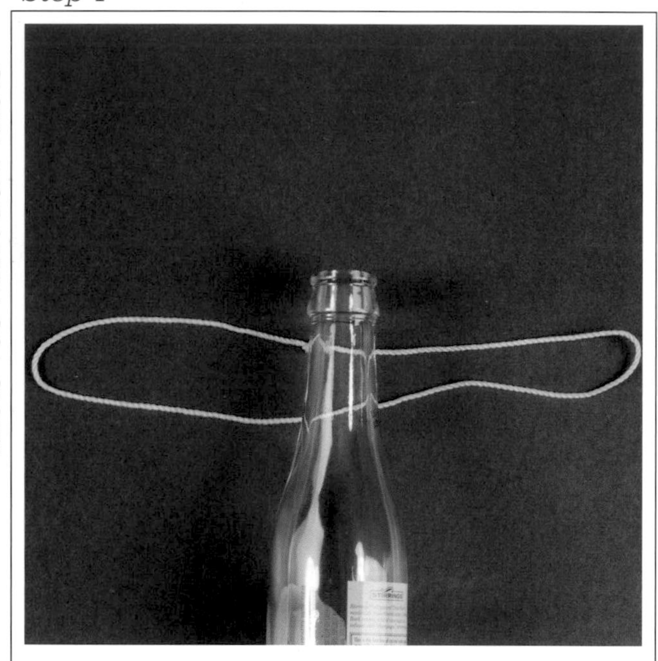

Begin by tying a piece of twine or cord into the appropriate-size loop. A fine knot for tying a loop is the double fisherman's knot (see page 108). Lay the loop beneath the neck of the bottle.

Asher's Bottle Sling: Step 2

Bring the bight on one side across the neck and through the bight on the other side, as shown in the photograph.

Sling knots may also be useful to anyone who wishes to secure a container of liquid for ease of carrying, hanging, or hauling. A climber, for instance, could use it to hang a water bottle from a climbing harness.

Asher's Bottle Sling: Step 3

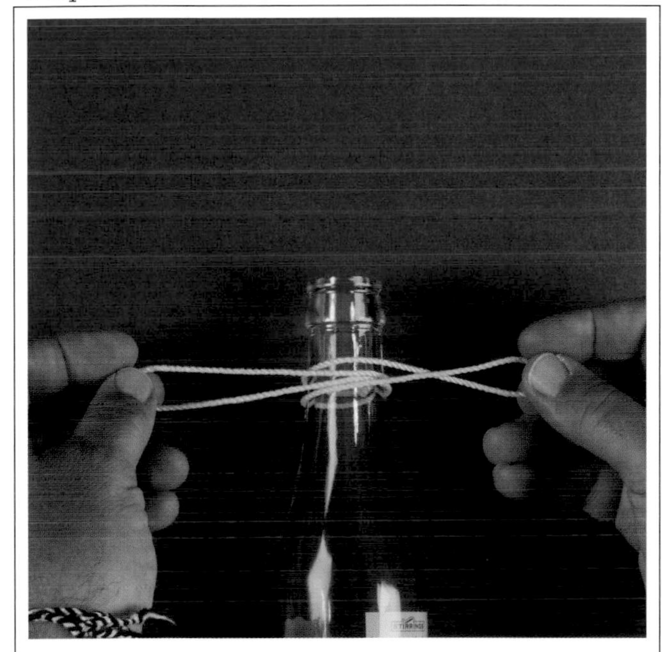

Bring the outer bight across the neck and give it a half twist into a loop.

Asher's Bottle Sling: Step 4

Bring the inner bight under the neck of the bottle and through the loop. Tighten by pulling on the inner bight and adjust the whole knot until it seats acceptably against the neck.

COMMON WHIPPING

Used to prevent a rope of several strands from fraying.

Whipping is the process of wrapping and seizing the end of a rope or line with strong, thin twine to prevent fraying. A frayed end is difficult to use and eventually leads to loss of a section of a typically expensive rope. When a rope is to be cut, always take steps to prevent fraying *before* cutting. Synthetic twine should be used on synthetic rope and natural fiber twine on natural fiber ropes. The common whipping is far from the most secure

Common Whipping: Step 1

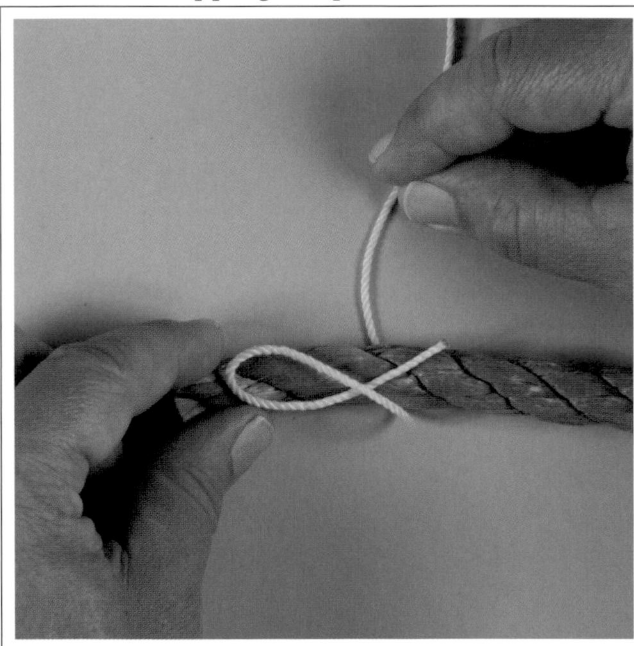

Lay a loop (or bight) of twine along the rope near the end.

Common Whipping: Step 2

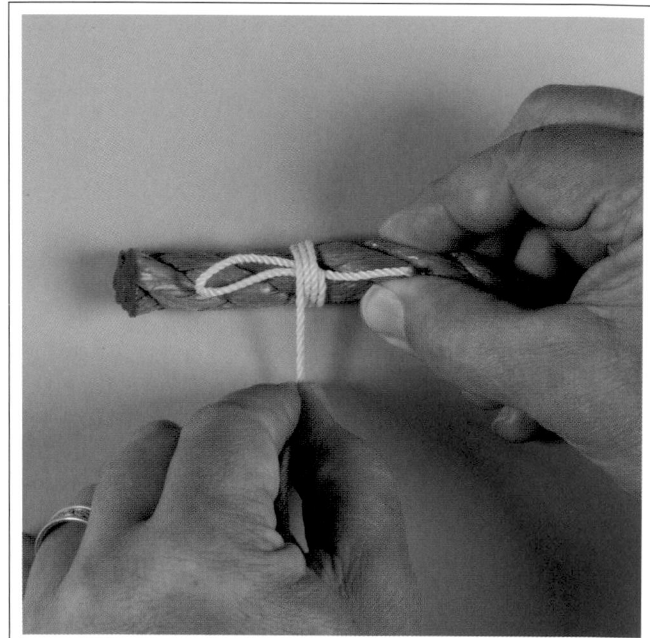

Wrap several turns of twine around the loop to bind it to the rope.

whipping, but it will work until a dependable whipping, usually sewn, can be acquired. Campers and climbers may need to use whipping to prevent a cut rope from fraying.

Make the turns of twine as tight as possible.

Common Whipping: Step 3

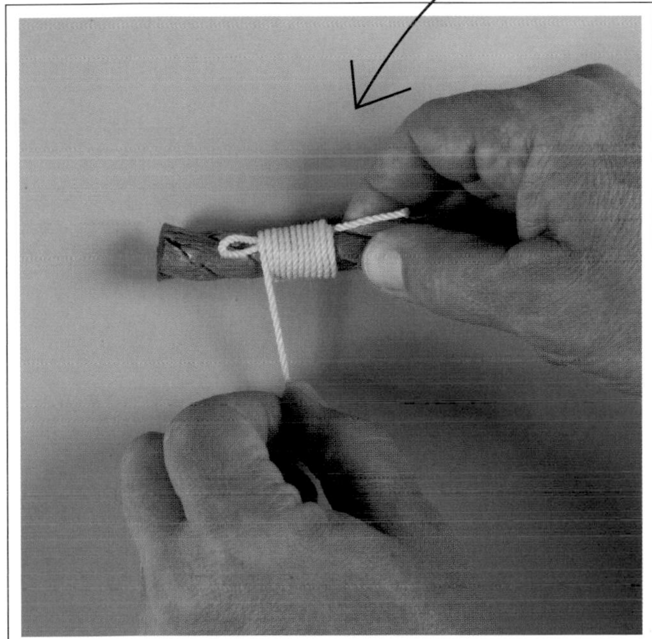

Continue binding the twine to the rope for a width greater than the diameter of the rope.

RED LIGHT

Some twines stretch when wet, allowing the whipping to slip off. Common whipping requires retying occasionally until a more secure whipping is acquired.

Common Whipping: Step 4

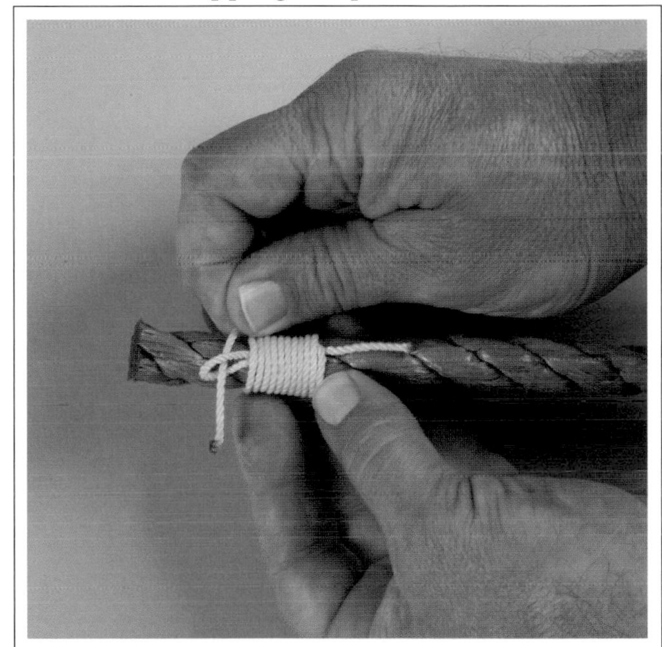

Tuck the working end through what is left of the loop and tighten by pulling on the stand ing part until the loop disappears beneath the binding.

BACHMANN HITCH

A friction knot for ascending a rope with a carabiner.

The Bachmann hitch attaches a carabiner to a rope with strong cord or webbing so that the carabiner can be used as a handle. Without a load, the hitch slides freely up the rope. Once weight is applied, the hitch grips the rope. The greater the difference between the diameter of the cord of the hitch and diameter of the main rope, the greater the grip of the hitch. This knot could be used to hang a load from a rope, in which case the weight should

Bachmann Hitch: Step 1

Attach a carabiner to a loop and place the loop around the rope, as shown in the photograph.

GREEN LIGHT

This knot might be used in camping to hang a food bag from a vertically suspended rope.

Bachmann Hitch: Step 2

Bring the end of the loop around the rope and through the carabiner.

be attached to the loop or sling, not to the carabiner, to prevent slipping.

The knot must finish with the loop pulled out through the carabiner.

Bachmann Hitch: Step 3

Bring the end of the loop around the rope and through the carabiner a second time.

Bachmann Hitch: Step 4

Bring the end of the loop around the rope and through the carabiner a third time. If the hitch does not grip adequately, you may add another turn of the loop.

GIRTH HITCH

Used for quickly attaching a loop to any object.

Simple and fast to apply, the girth hitch (or ring hitch) has many uses. It attaches a pre-sewn or pre-tied loop or sling to any fixed object. It can be used to connect loops or attach a loop to a climbing harness from which gear can be hung. Climbers often use a girth hitch in slings of webbing, but it works in any type of rope or cordage.

The knot that ties the cord into a loop should be positioned to the side of the loop, not at the bottom where it could get in the way.

Girth Hitch: Step 1

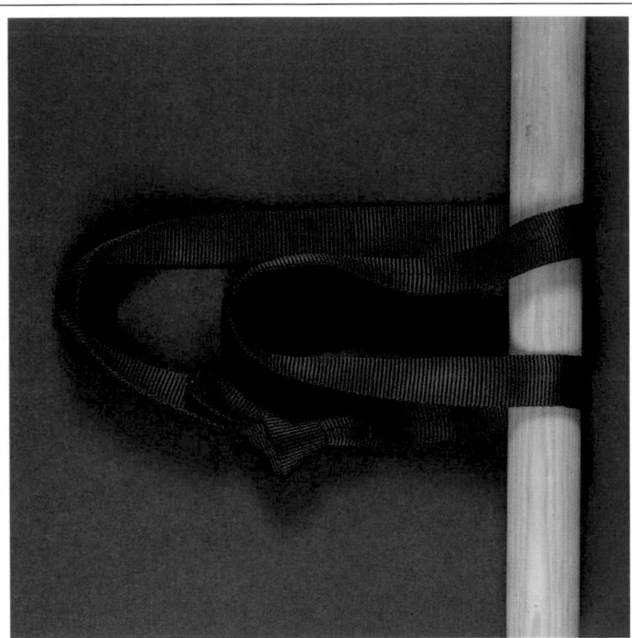

Pass the loop around the object to which it is to be attached.

GREEN LIGHT

This knot is often used in camping and could be helpful to boaters for numerous jobs, such as creating loops from which gear can be hung.

Girth Hitch: Step 2

Bring one half of the loop through the other half, and tighten by pulling on the lower half.

MUNTER (ITALIAN) HITCH

Used for improvising a belay or a rappel device with the use of one or two carabiners.

The Munter hitch works as a climbing device for belaying and rappelling and should be learned by all climbers. The knot grips a carabiner when a load is applied, but the rope runs freely through the carabiner when the load is off. It should be used with one locking carabiner or two non-locking carabiners with the gates reversed.

ZOOM

Werner Munter, a Swiss guide, popularized this knot, leaving his name in the annals of climbing.

Munter Hitch: Step 1

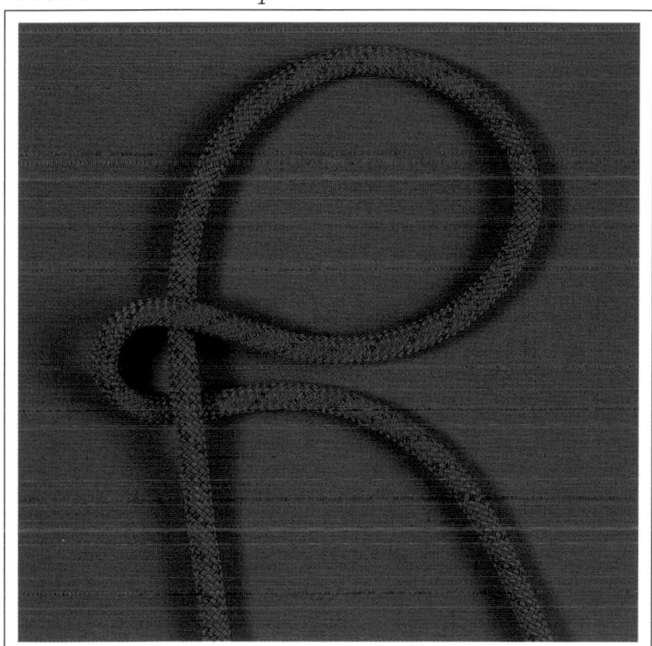

Twist a coil into the rope with the upper and lower strands of the coil folded together, as shown in the photograph.

RED LIGHT

Test the knot on safe ground by pulling aggressively on the standing part before trusting it to save a life!

Munter Hitch: Step 2

Clip the carabiner into both sides of the folded strand with the spine of the carabiner next to the strand that will bear the load.

GARDA KNOT

A ratcheting knot that employs two carabiners and is useful in hauling.

The Garda knot ratchets, allowing the rope to pass through a pair of carabiners in one direction only. The two carabiners should be the same size and shape, and they should not be locking carabiners since the locks prevent them from pinching the rope firmly enough for the knot to work. This knot might also be useful in camping.

RED LIGHT

If the rope rides up onto the gates, the Garda may come unclipped. This can be prevented by maintaining tension on the rope.

Garda Knot: Step 1

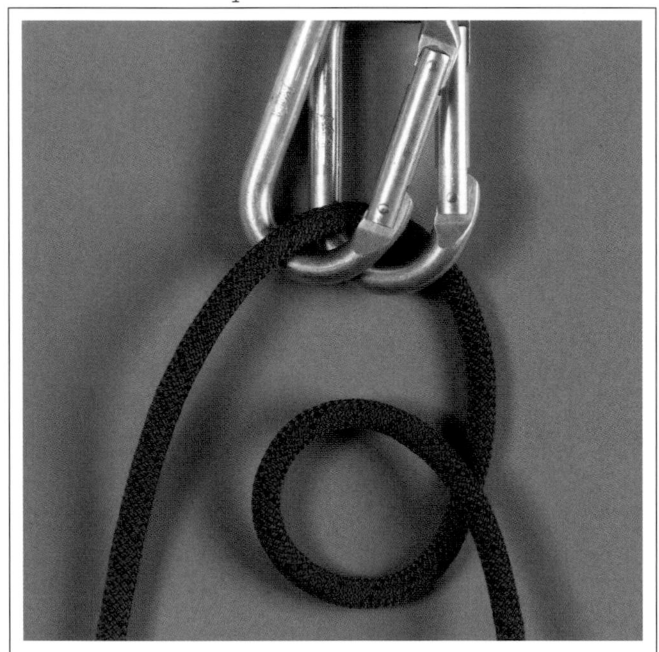

Clip two carabiners into a sling, side by side, with the gates facing in the same direction. Pass the rope through both carabiners and form a loop, as shown in the photograph.

Garda Knot: Step 2

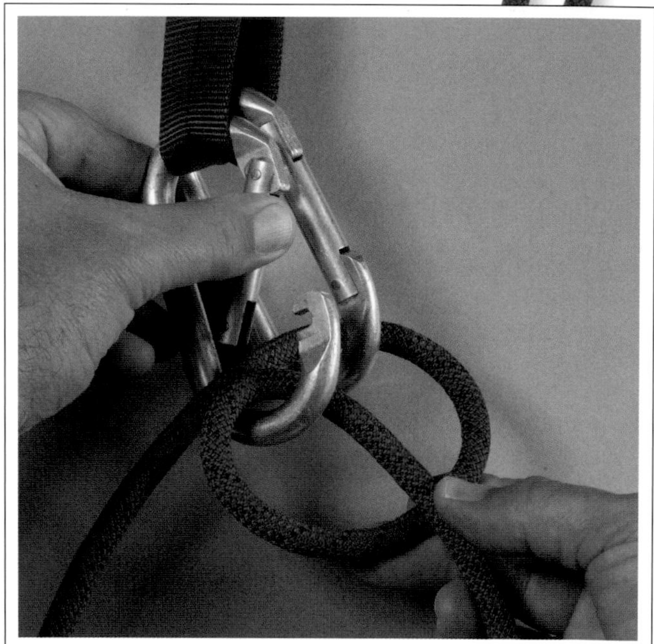

Pass the loop through the first carabiner only. Slide the loop onto the spines of the carabiners, the sides opposite to the gates, before loading the system.

KLEMHEIST KNOT

A friction knot for ascending a rope or escaping a belay.

When tied properly, the klemheist knot grips the rope when weighted but releases and slides along the rope when the load is off. It releases and slides with more ease than the Prusik knot (see page 102) but grips with less tenacity than the Prusik. It works well for tying off a climber's rope to allow escape from the belay.

Klemheist Knot: Step 1

Wrap a loop of cord or a sling of webbing four or five times around the rope and toward the load, keeping the wraps neatly laid against the rope.

Klemheist Knot: Step 2

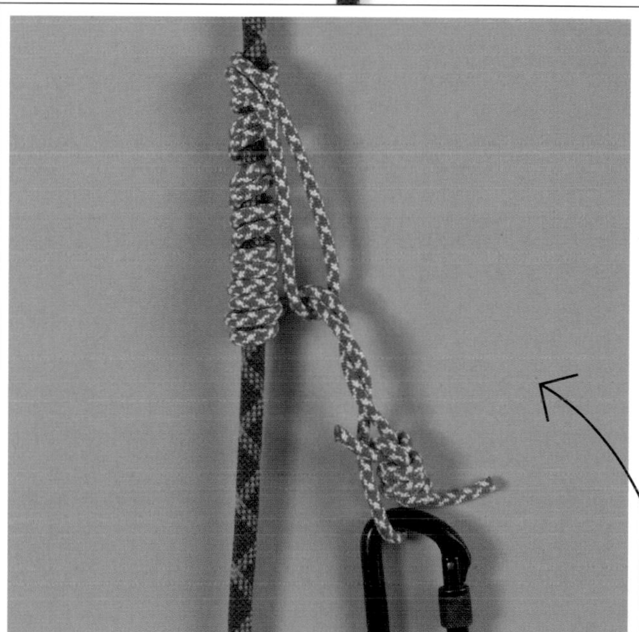

Pass the lower end of the loop through the upper end and clip a carabiner into the lower loop.

Add more wraps if the knot slips.

PRUSIK KNOT

A friction knot used for ascending a rope.

As with the klemheist knot (see page 101), the Prusik slides up the rope when unloaded but grips the rope firmly when loaded. A big difference, however, is in the fact that the Prusik grips the rope better, so much so that it may be difficult to break free after being loaded with a heavy weight. But it can be broken free by loosening the "tongue" (center loop) first. This knot is a better choice for new, wet, or otherwise slippery rope.

The word *prusik* may be used to refer not only to the knot but also to the loop of cord in which the knot is tied

Prusik Knot: Step 1

Tie a loop in a cord of significantly smaller diameter than the main rope.

GREEN LIGHT

This knot might be used in camping for such tasks as hanging bags on ropes suspended vertically to keep the bags out of animal reach.

Prusik Knot: Step 2

Girth hitch (see page 98) the loop to the main rope, keeping the hitch loose.

and to the ascending technique "to prusik". With practice, the Prusik knot can be tied with one hand, a useful skill in an emergency when the other hand may be unavailable. Many climbers today utilize mechanical ascenders instead of the Prusik knot. Mechanical ascenders damage a rope more than the Prusik, but the Prusik will fail (slip) if it is overloaded, a problem rarely seen with mechanical devices.

Prusik Knot: Step 3

Bring the loop around the rope and back through the hitch a second time.

Test the knot, and if it slips add more wraps.

Prusik Knot: Step 4

Bring the loop around and through a third time. Lay the wraps of loop evenly and with out twists to maximize the bite on the rope. Tighten the knot against the rope.

ROUND TURN & TWO HALF HITCHES

A variation of two half hitches that creates a knot of unparalleled strength.

Not only strong and dependable, this knot, when tied correctly, never jams. Because weight applied to the standing part pulls the rope in a straight line, the breaking strength is not diminished by the round turn and two half hitches. It is useful for securing one end of a rope when the other end will be used to fasten down bulky objects.

Round Turn and Two Half Hitches: Step 1

Take the working end of the rope around an object in a full round turn.

GREEN LIGHT

This knot is used in climbing, boating, and fishing.

Remember to tighten the first half hitch before tying the second.

Round Turn and Two Half Hitches: Step 2

Tie two half hitches (see page 35) in the working end.

HUNTER'S (RIGGER'S) BEND

Used for joining two ropes in a tight, strong, and secure-when-loaded knot.

Based on the interweaving of two overhand knots, the Hunter's bend is quickly and easily learned. It tightens securely when loaded, but it can be worked loose and separated when the load is off.

BENDS

Tie an overhand knot at the working end of the first rope but do not tighten it.

This knot is used in camping, boating, and, in fact, any activity in which the joining of two ropes is needed.

Thread the working end of the second rope through the loop of the overhand knot in the first rope. Bring the end of the second rope around and back through the loop of the first overhand a second time, forming an overhand knot in the second rope, as shown in the photograph. Tighten.

FISHERMAN'S KNOT

A simple, quick-tying knot for joining two ropes of similar diameter.

One of the most common bends used by climbers, the compact fisherman's knot combines two overhand knots that jam against each other when pressure is applied. Simple to tie even with cold, wet hands, this knot has earned its popularity—and it works well in the stiffest cordage. It unties fairly easily, even after being weighted, but it can bind up after being shock-loaded. The knot works best in ropes of similar thickness and, therefore, does a fine job of tying two ends of the same rope together.

Since it works very well in lines of very small diameter,

Fisherman's Knot: Step 1

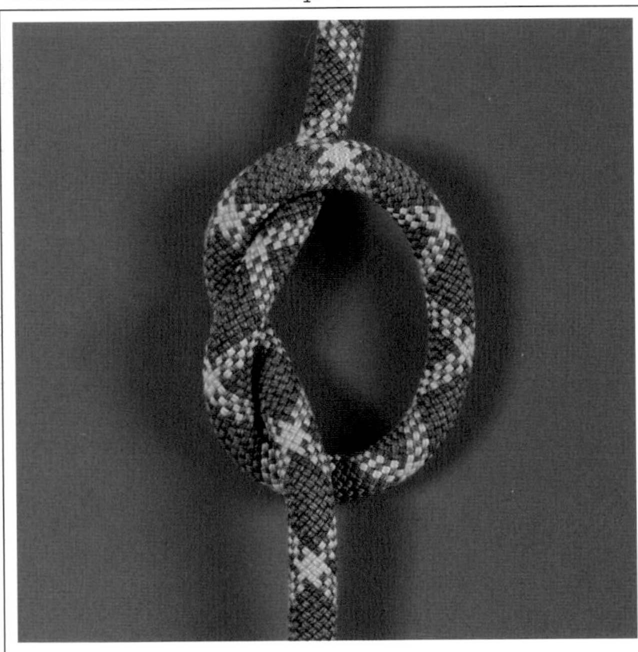

Form an overhand knot at the working end of the first rope.

GREEN LIGHT

This knot is used in camping, boating, and, of course, fishing.

Fisherman's Knot: Step 2

Thread the working end of the second rope through the overhand knot in the first rope, as shown in the photograph.

such as fishing line, it is popular with anglers, so much so the knot bears their name. But fishermen called this knot the water knot in the 1600s and 1700s, later referring to it as the angler's knot. It has also been called the English knot, the Englishman's knot, the waterman's knot, and the true lover's knot.

Fisherman's Knot: Step 3

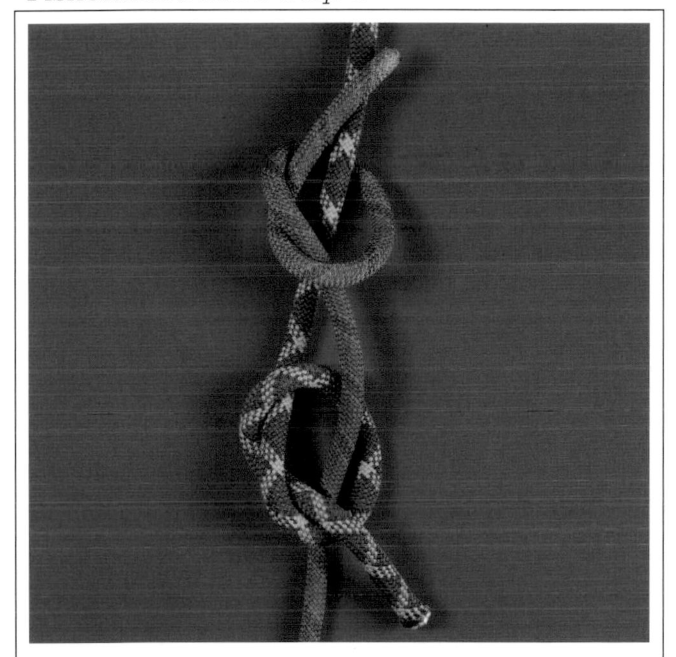

Tie an overhand knot in the working end of the second rope. The second overhand must be tied around the first rope, as shown in the photograph.

Fisherman's Knot: Step 4

Tighten both overhand knots and draw them together slowly by pulling on the standing parts of both ropes.

DOUBLE FISHERMAN'S KNOT

One of the safest, most secure knots for joining two ropes of similar diameter.

As the name implies, the double fisherman's knot extends the fisherman's knot (see page 106), joining two ropes or lines of similar size in an extremely secure knot. In the double fisherman's, two double overhand knots jam against each other when pressure is applied. It is an excellent choice when using synthetic cordage, including fishing line. It works in natural fiber cordage, of course, but it can become extremely difficult to untie from anything other than synthetics.

After being weighted, the two double overhands form

Double Fisherman's Knot: Step 1

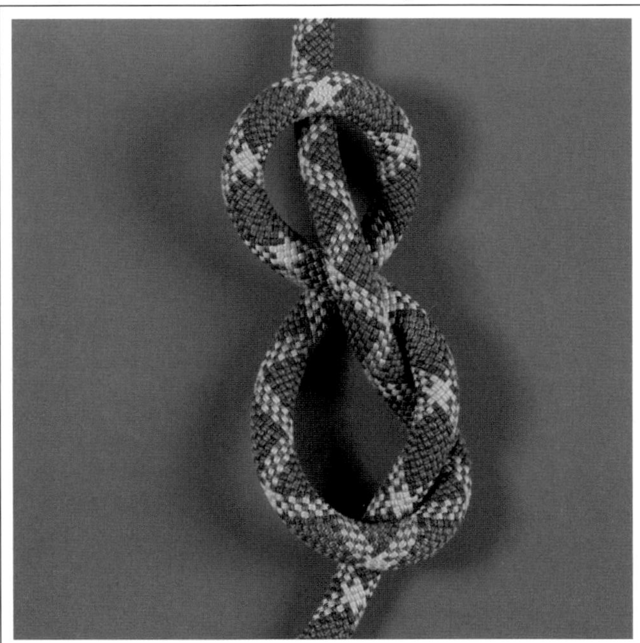

Form a double overhand knot (see page 52) at the working end of the first rope.

Double Fisherman's Knot: Step 2

Thread the working end of the second rope through both loops of the double overhand knot in the first rope, as shown in the photograph.

a tight bond that simply stays put. For this reason, climbers will use this knot to create a short sling or loop to aid climbing. Fishermen often call the double fisherman's knot the grinner knot for reasons not completely understood. Perhaps it's because it looks, to some, like open mouths prior to being tightened.

Double Fisherman's Knot: Step 3

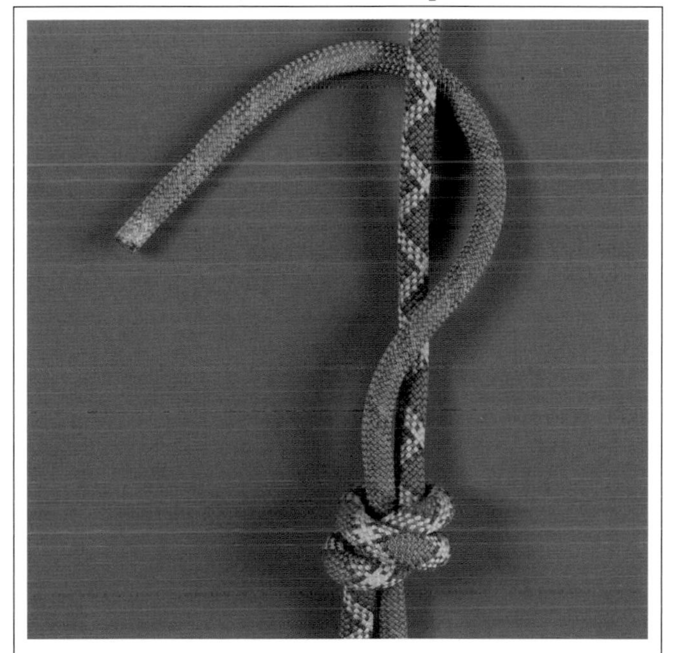

Tighten the double overhand in the first rope.

At this point it will be easier to continue if you reverse the knot assembly in your hand.

Double Fisherman's Knot: Step 4

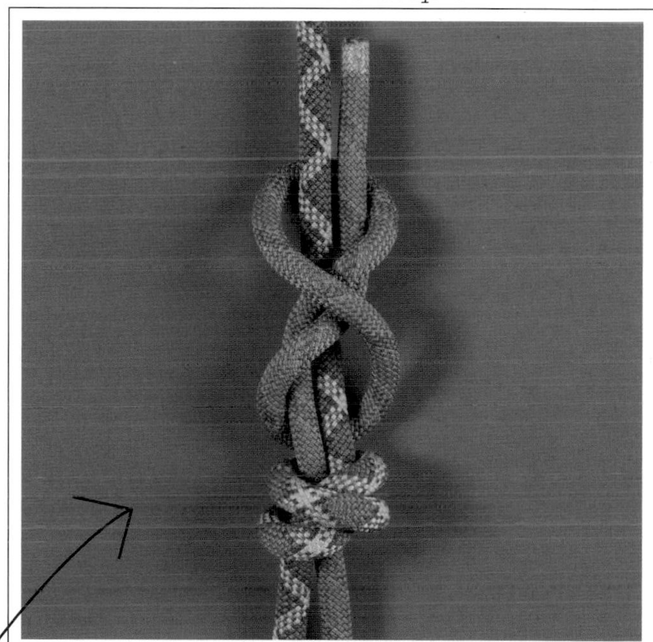

Form a double overhand in the working end of the second rope, making sure both loops of the knot are around the standing part of the first rope. Tighten the second double overhand and draw both knots together slowly by pulling on the standing part of both ropes.

WATER KNOT

Joins two ends of a length of tubular nylon webbing into a loop or two lengths of webbing.

Most climbers today use webbing sewn into slings by a manufacturer. Webbing is nylon woven stoutly into a tubular shape, then flattened. If, however, you need to tie a sling or loop, or tie two lengths of webbing together, the relatively simple water knot works well. It is created by weaving two overhand knots together, one the mirror image of the other. It can be tied in any material, including rope and fishing line. Although this knot creates a very secure bend in cord, twine, and monofilaments, it almost always tightens irretrievably in small lines.

Water Knot: Step 1

Form an overhand knot in the end of the webbing, making sure the webbing is arranged to allow the knot to lie flat if pressed.

Water Knot: Step 2

Slide the second end of webbing into the first overhand knot, as if you're tracing the knot. Start at the point where the first end of webbing leaves the first overhand knot, as shown in the photograph.

Webbing is known as tape to some, and this knot is called by those same people the tape knot. Hutton's *Dictionary*, published in 1815, referred to this knot as the ring knot, and it may also be known as the ring bend. Older publications call it the gut knot, an indication that it has been around a long time, certainly long before synthetic lines.

RED LIGHT

Water knots have a tendency to creep apart and should be used in climbing with at least 3 inches of tail on both ends and/or with the tails fixed with adhesive tape.

BENDS

Water Knot: Step 3

Continue to follow the lead of the first piece of webbing through the overhand knot with the second end of webbing, making sure both ends of webbing lie flat against each other.

Water Knot: Step 4

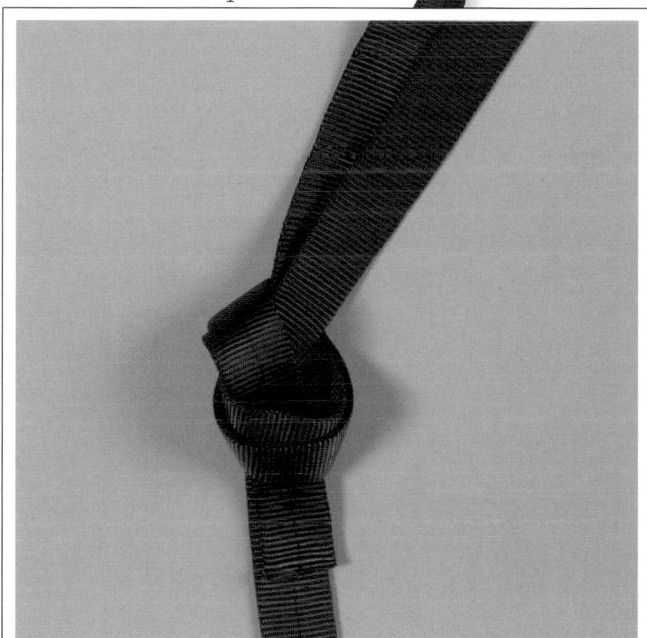

When both ends of webbing have been woven into one overhand knot, tighten it by pulling on the working ends of the webbing. Before trusting the knot to stop a fall, load it with body weight to set it as tight as possible.

FIGURE 8 BEND

A more complex knot used for securely joining two ropes of similar size and construction.

The figure 8 bend is created by weaving together two figure 8 knots. Climbers tend to prefer this bend because of its security as well as the strength of the interwoven working ends. If heavily loaded, this knot may prove impossible to untie if the ropes are of approximately the same diameter. It does hold nearly as well in ropes of dissimilar diameter. Despite its security, climbers often leave the working ends long enough to back up the knot with stoppers, adding even more security (not a bad idea when your life may depend on your knot).

Figure 8 Bend: Step 1

Tie a figure 8 knot (see page 22) in the working end of one rope.

Figure 8 Bend: Step 2

Thread the working end of the second rope into the figure 8 knot in the first rope, as shown in the photograph.

Clifford Ashley, arguably the greatest knot-man of all times, called the figure 8 bend a Flemish bend and found it, reportedly, a bothersome knot to deal with. This knot may also be used by campers and boaters.

For the greatest strength, make sure the standing part of both ropes forms the outer bight at both ends of the knot.

Figure 8 Bend: Step 3

Continue to follow the lead of the first rope. The goal is to create a second figure 8 knot that duplicates the first figure 8 knot.

Figure 8 Bend: Step 4

When both ropes have been woven into one figure 8 knot, carefully compress and tighten the composite knot into the characteristic figure 8 shape.

FIGURE 8 FOLLOW-THROUGH

A fixed loop, the standard tie-in knot for climbers.

Since the tie-in knot is where a climber is attached to a climbing rope, it is of critical importance. The figure 8 follow-through is most often chosen. If you can know only one knot well, beginning climbers are often told, the figure 8 follow-through is the one.

It is not only a strong and secure loop but easy to visually inspect for correctness. The working end follows the path of the rope through a figure 8 that has already been tied, and thus the name. The figure 8 follow-through is no more than a figure 8 loop (see page 28), but it is tied

Figure 8 Follow-Through: Step 1

Tie a figure 8 knot (see page 22) in the working end of the rope.

You will need the figure 8 knot to be 2 to 3 feet from the working end.

Figure 8 Follow-Through: Step 2

With the working end, begin to trace, or follow the lead of, the first figure 8, as shown in the photograph.

differently—in this case the loop being tied around an object, most often the climber's harness. Sometimes called the Flemish bend, it is not a bend—the Flemish bend being another name for the figure 8 bend, a knot for tying two different ropes together. This knot may also be used by campers and boaters.

RED●LIGHT

Before trusting this knot to save your life, leave enough working end to back up the knot with a stopper. The double overhand (see page 52) is an excellent choice.

Figure 8 Follow-Through: Step 3

Continue to follow the lead of the figure 8.

Figure 8 Follow-Through: Step 4

The working end needs to come out of the knot in line with the standing part, as shown in the photograph.

FIGURE 8 DOUBLE LOOP

A variation of the figure 8 that creates twin loops in the rope.

The figure 8 double loop (sometimes called "bunny ears") creates twin loops that allow a climber to secure one rope to two anchors. Once mastered, this knot ties quickly and forms two secure fixed loops that will not alter in size when weight is applied to either or both loops. If loops of differing sizes are needed, however, the loops can be adjusted to different sizes during the tying—and they too will remain secure.

As with the double bowline (see page 66), the figure 8 double loop could be used in an emergency as a chair

Figure 8 Double Loop: Step 1

Form a large bight in the rope and twist the bight into a loop as if starting a simple figure 8 (see page 28).

GREEN ● LIGHT

This knot is also used in camping and boating.

Figure 8 Double Loop: Step 2

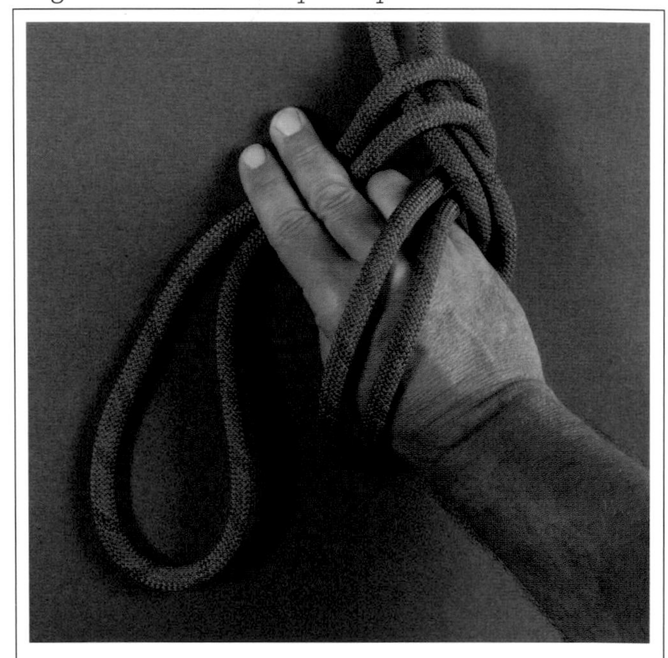

Reach through the loop and grasp the doubled rope, as shown in the photograph.

sling to raise or lower a person if, of course, the loops are made large enough. When used as a chair sling, both knots share the common characteristic of being highly uncomfortable. This knot was first described in print in 1944 by Clifford Ashley. How long it was in use prior to Ashley's description is not known.

The doubled section of rope pulled through the loop will become the double loop.

Figure 8 Double Loop: Step 3

Bring the doubled rope through the loop as if tying a figure 8 with draw loop (see page 24).

Figure 8 Double Loop: Step 4

Bring the remaining single loop down in front of the knot, take the doubled loops through the single loop, and move the single loop up to the top of the knot. Carefully tighten everything.

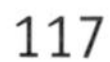

FIGURE 8 TRIPLE LOOP

A variation of the figure 8 that creates three loops in the rope.

The figure 8 triple loop (sometimes called the triple figure 8 loop) creates three loops that allow a climber to secure one rope to three anchors. Once mastered, this knot ties quickly and forms three secure fixed loops that will not alter in size once the final knot is tightened. As with the triple bowline (see page 68), the figure 8 triple loop could be used, in an emergency, as a chair sling to raise or lower a person with one loop for each leg and the

Figure 8 Triple Loop: Step 1

Form a large bight in the rope and twist the bight into a loop as if starting a simple figure 8 (see page 28).

GREEN ● LIGHT

This knot may be used by campers and boaters who want to attach three objects to the end of one rope.

Figure 8 Triple Loop: Step 2

Reach through the loop and grasp the doubled rope. Bring the doubled rope through the loop as if tying a figure 8 with draw loop (see page 24). You are now at a point where you could tie a figure 8 double loop (see page 116).

third loop around the torso beneath the armpits. Though not recommended except in extreme circumstances, it could be used to lower an unconscious person.

These three loops are smaller than most climbers would need but are shown small for photographic purposes.

Figure 8 Triple Loop: Step 3

Bring the remaining single loop over the top of the knot.

Figure 8 Triple Loop: Step 4

Bring this loop down through the original loop to create three loops. Carefully tighten everything.

ALPINE BUTTERFLY

Forms a fixed loop in the standing part of a rope.

This knot with the loveliest of names creates a fixed loop at any point in a rope, a loop to which anything may be clipped or otherwise attached. It is often used in climbing as a knot to which a climber may be attached to the rope. It is especially popular in glacier travel, where it is common to find three climbers attached to one rope, one climber at each end and one in the middle.

Unlike the loop knot (see page 126), the alpine butterfly can and safely does serve to bear a critical load. It stands up to tension from either direction without weakening.

Alpine Butterfly: Step 1

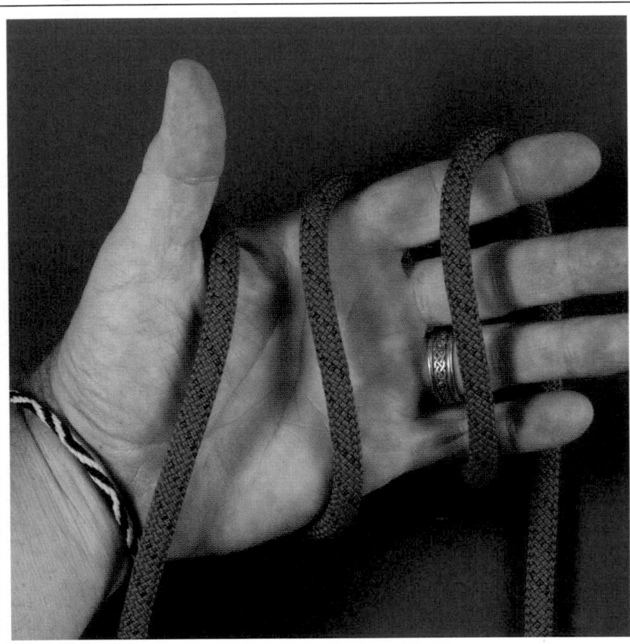

Wrap the rope around your left hand twice, as shown in the photograph.

Alpine Butterfly: Step 2

Move the turn closest to your fingertips to lie between the other two turns.

In addition to strength and security, the alpine butterfly almost always unties easily, even after being heavily loaded, something other loops fail to do. As with other loops, this knot can be used to isolate—within the loop of the knot—a worn or otherwise weakened point of a

By grasping the loop, you can now remove the rope from your hand.

Alpine Butterfly: Step 3

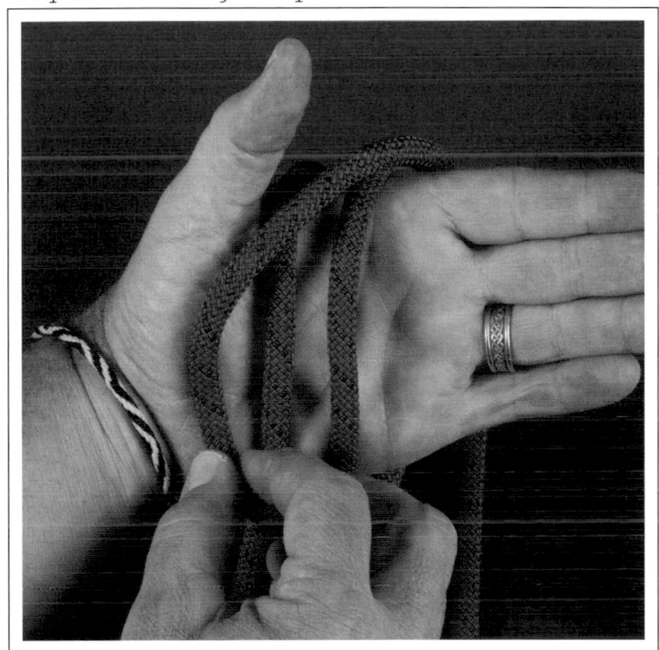

Move the turn that is now closest to your fingertips to lie closest to your thumb.

Alpine Butterfly: Step 4

Bring the turn now closest to your thumb underneath the other two turns toward your fingertips.

rope. It is occasionally called the lineman's knot or lineman's loop.

As with so many members of the knot world, this one can be tied in several ways. This way is relatively easy to visualize.

Alpine Butterfly: Step 5

Shape the knot by pulling on the loop and the two main sections of the rope.

GREEN ● LIGHT

This knot may be used in camping, boating, and fishing, or any time an object needs to be attached to a rope at a point other than the end.

Alpine Butterfly: Step 6

Tighten the knot by pulling on the two main sections of the rope.

SPANISH BOWLINE

Two separate and independent fixed loops useful in mountain rescue work.

The Spanish bowline, also known as the chair knot, is a very strong knot. It is safe and holds securely even under a great load. It can be used to hoist large, heavy objects, such as equipment. In rescue work one loop goes over a person's head and down under the armpits, the other loop around the legs behind the knees, allowing an

GREEN LIGHT

This knot has been useful to boaters as a means of lowering an injured sailor over the side and into another boat.

Spanish Bowline: Step 1

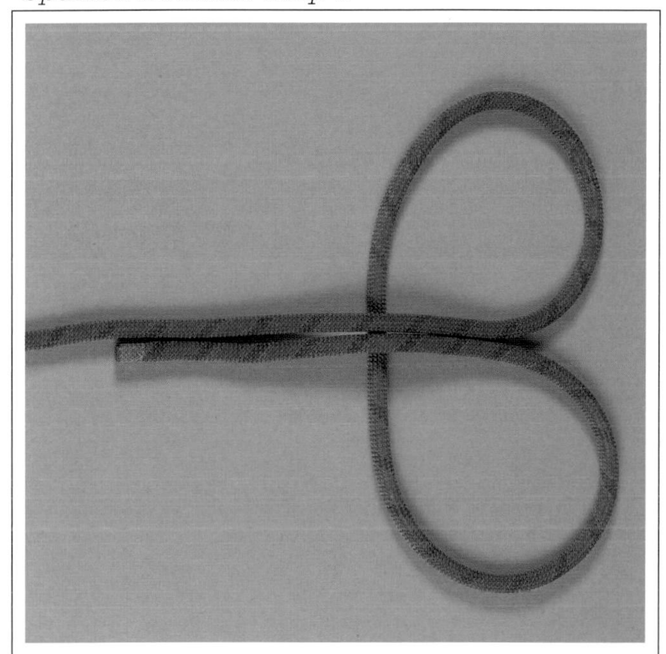

Form two loops in the working end of the rope, as shown in the photograph.

Spanish Bowline: Step 2

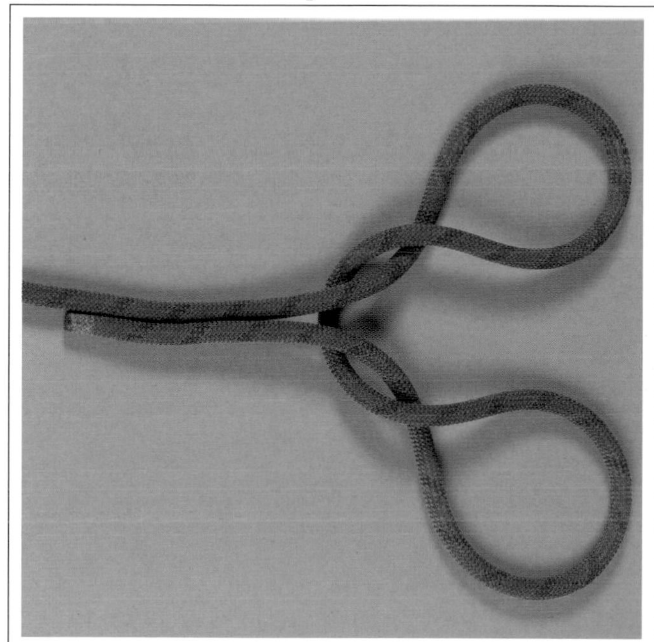

Twist each loop separately toward the center of the knot.

LOOPS

unconscious person to be lowered. For use with a conscious person, one loop goes around each leg and the person being lowered holds onto the rope. The loops are easy to adjust during tying since the rope moves freely through the knot.

On the downside, the ease of adjustment of the loops means the final knot must be set very tight before use or the loops could alter in size when the knot is weighted. Since better methods of attaching people to ropes have been developed, such as pre-sewn chairs, it is not recommended to use the Spanish bowline as a chair except in emergencies. Knotmaster Clifford Ashley referred to this knot by the unwieldy name of a double splayed loop in the bight.

Spanish Bowline: Step 3

Reach through the right-hand loop and grasp the left-hand loop.

Spanish Bowline: Step 4

Bring the left loop through the right loop.

These loops are smaller than most climbers would need but are shown small for photographic purposes. Have patience when adjusting the final loops, as this will need practice.

Spanish Bowline: Step 5

Reach through both loops simultaneously (using both hands) and grasp the points of the newly formed lower loop at the top, where indicated in the photograph.

Spanish Bowline: Step 6

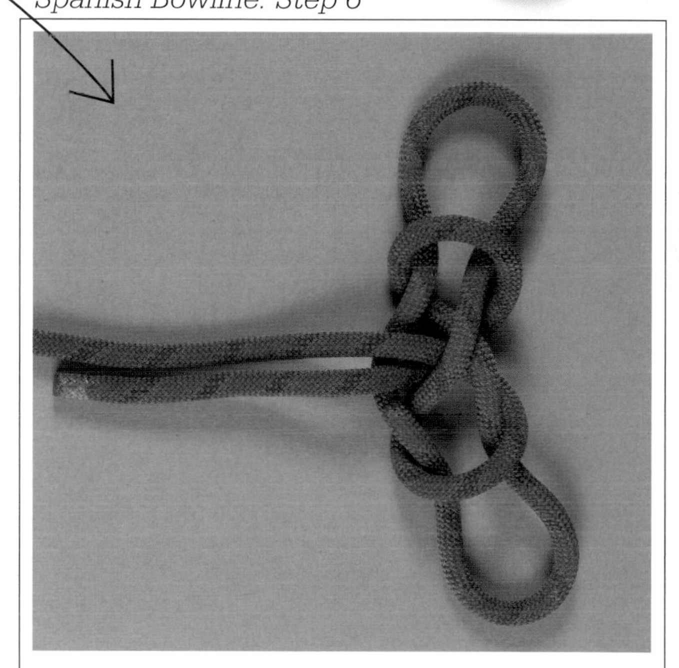

Bring the two points indicated out through the upper loops to form two new loops. Painstakingly adjust the final loops to the required size and pull strongly on the central knot to tighten.

LOOP KNOT

The quickest and simplest loop in the middle of a rope, and for emergency "repair" of a damaged rope.

When something needs to be attached mid-rope, the loop knot works well. This knot is important for shortening and keeping a damaged rope functional. With the damaged part in the middle of the knot, it is put under no strain. The loop, however, should not bear critical weight.

A damaged section of a rope would be at the top of the bight.

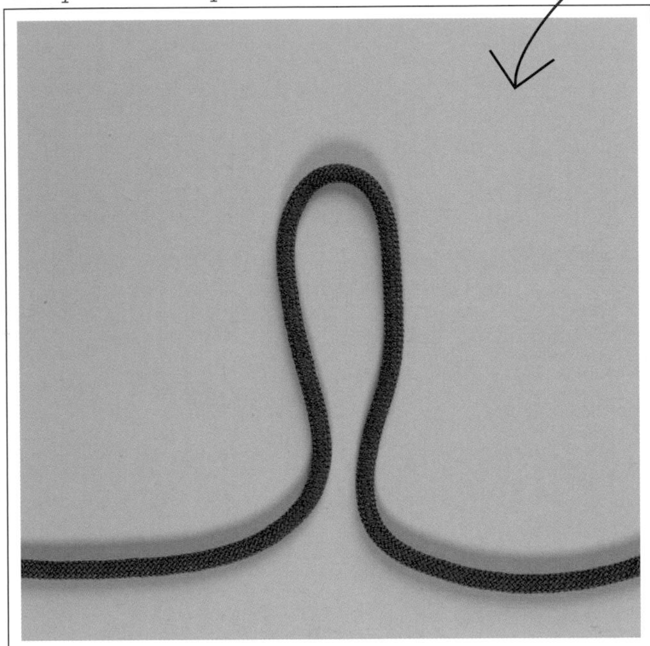

Form a bight in the rope.

Any damaged climbing rope needs to be replaced as soon as possible. Using a knot to "strengthen" a damaged rope is an emergency measure to prevent the rope from failing before the climb has ended.

Loop Knot: Step 2

Tie an overhand knot (see page 18) in the bight. Tighten by pulling slowly on the loop and the main sections of the rope.

ARBOR KNOT

A knot that attaches one end of the line to the arbor of the reel.

Any sliding loop that attaches the fishing line to the arbor (spindle) of the reel is known as an arbor knot (or reel knot). When the knot is tightened, it jams against the arbor, allowing the remainder of the line to be spooled onto the reel.

Arbor Knot: Step 1

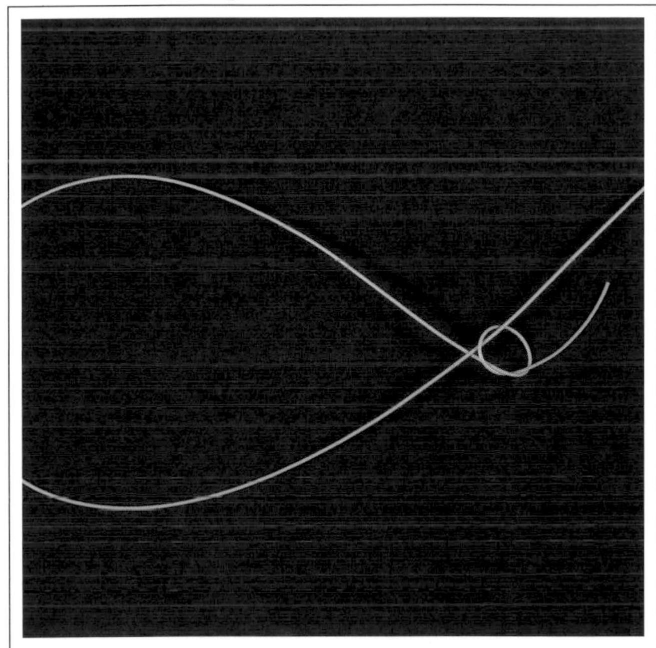

Take the line around the arbor of the reel (not shown in the photograph) and tie the working end around the line in an overhand knot (see page 18).

Arbor Knot: Step 2

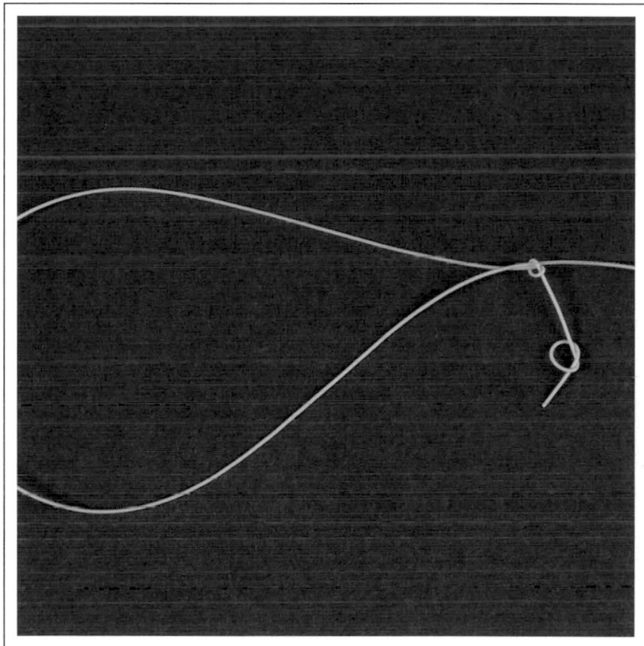

Tie a second overhand knot in the working end. When the standing part is pulled, the knots will jam together against the arbor.

IMPROVED CLINCH KNOT

A knot used for attaching hook or fly to line.

The improved clinch knot (also known as the clinch knot or the half blood knot) adds a second tuck of the line to increase the grip of the original clinch knot. It is a trusted knot, a favorite of anglers around the world.

Fishing, however, is a sport filled with strong preferences, and some anglers cling to the original clinch knot as their favorite, saying the improved clinch knot fails to be stronger. But tied correctly, the improved clinch knot

Improved Clinch Knot: Step 1

Thread the line through the eye of the hook or fly and make five turns of the line around itself (or less turns in a heavier line).

Improved Clinch Knot: Step 2

Tuck the working end through the small loop in the line near the eye.

is an improvement over the original, giving better grip between line and hook. It works in the finest monofilament but may prove a bit slippery in heavy line, where it sometimes resists complete tightening. This is a pure angling knot with no other known uses.

ZOOM

All fishing knots tighten easier and more firmly when the line is wet. Dip the knot in water before tightening.

Improved Clinch Knot: Step 3

Tuck the working end through the loop created when the line was tucked through the small loop near the eye.

Improved Clinch Knot: Step 4

Pull on both the hook or fly and the standing part to tighten the knot against the eye. Trim off the tag end, the short length of the working end that remains after tightening.

DRY FLY KNOT

A knot used for attaching a fly to the tippet.

Although it is called the dry fly knot, this knot works well with any fly, dry or not, and works especially well when the eye is tipped up or down. It is photographed in a hook with a flat end for better visibility. When tied properly, this knot does not reduce the strength of the tippet. It prevents the fly from cocking or tipping on the end of the tippet, allowing the fly to float realistically in the water.

Dry Fly Knot: Step 1

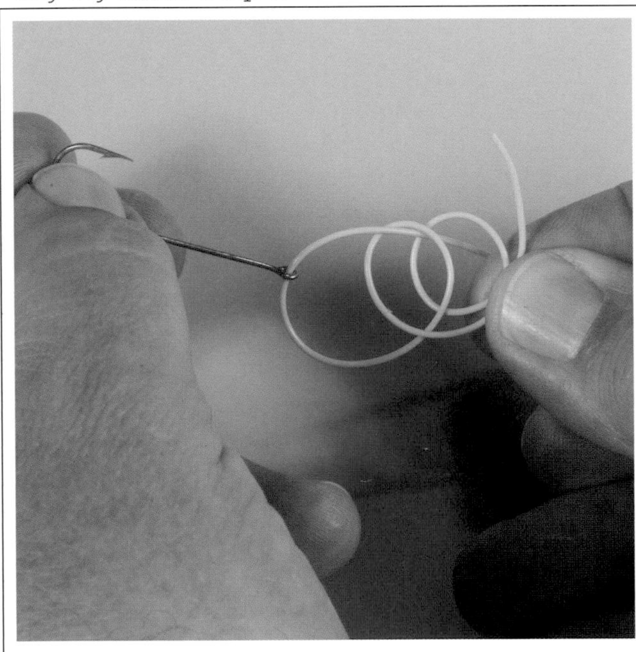

Thread the tippet through the eye of the fly and make two turns of the line around itself, as shown in the photograph.

Dry Fly Knot: Step 2

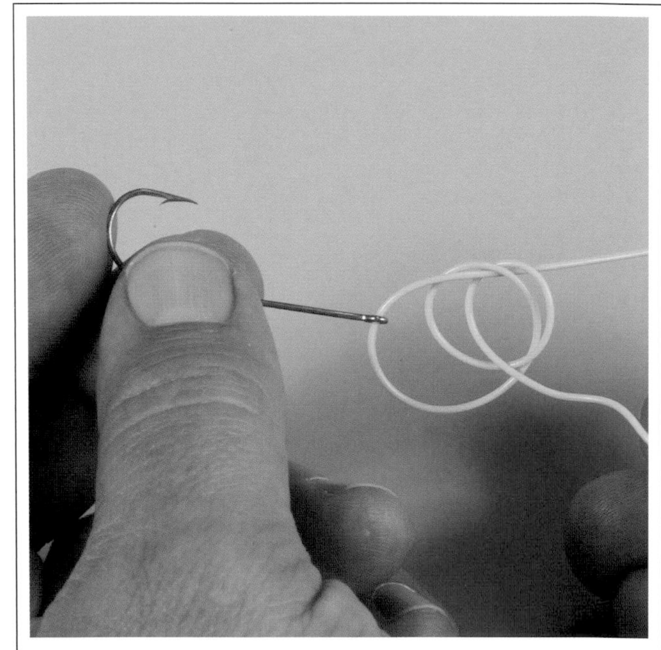

Tuck the working end through the two loops, as shown in the photograph.

George Harvey, a Pennsylvania outdoorsman extraordinaire, sometimes called the Dean of Fly Fishing, has devoted his life to fishing and to educating others in the art of fishing. He is credited with the invention of this knot. It is another pure angling knot.

Dry Fly Knot: Step 3

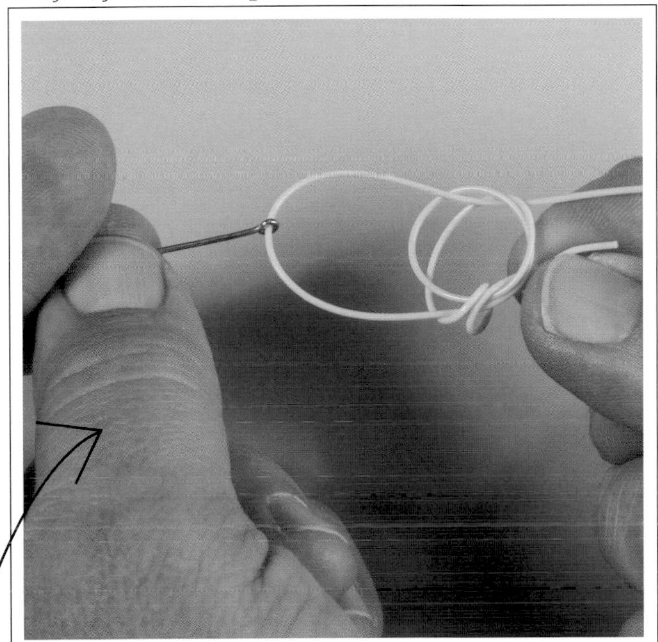

Tuck the working end through the two loops a second time.

Have patience when working with smaller knots. Tying the perfect knot takes practice.

Dry Fly Knot: Step 4

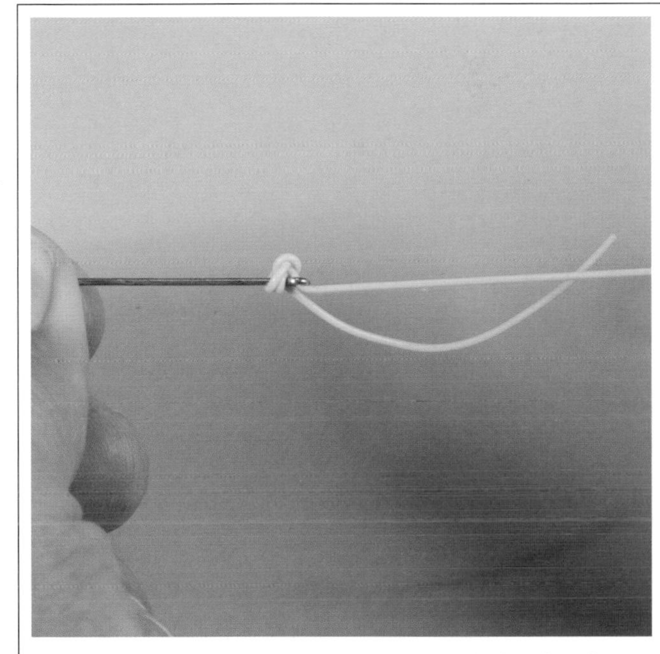

Pull on the standing part and slide the knot up onto the shank of the fly hook. Tighten the knot and trim off the tag end.

UNI-KNOT

One of the most universal fishing knots.

The universal knot, or uni-knot, meets just about any situation in fresh or saltwater fishing. Sometimes known as the grinner knot, it is not a difficult knot to tie once it has been mastered. Tying knots of this size takes practice and patience. It can be used to snell a hook (see page 142); to tie a hook, lure, swivel, or sinker to just about any type of line; or to tie a line to the arbor of a reel.

This knot is credited to Vic Dunaway, who developed

Uni-Knot: Step 1

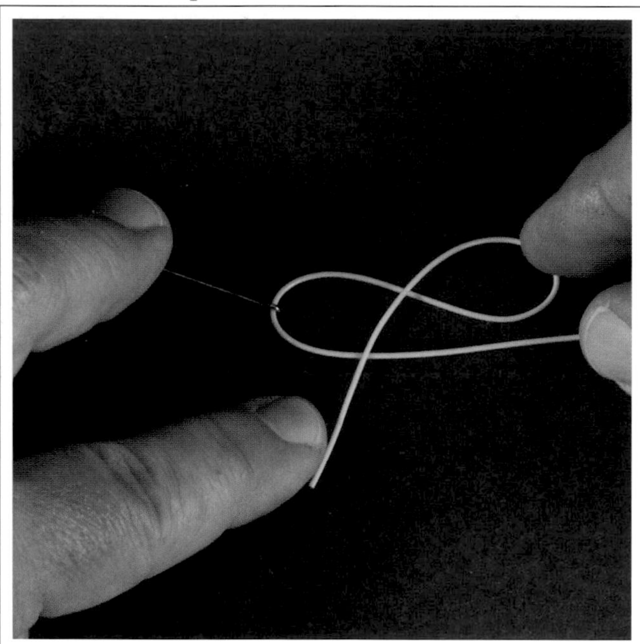

Thread the line through the eye of the hook and form a loop back toward the eye, as shown in the photograph.

Uni-Knot: Step 2

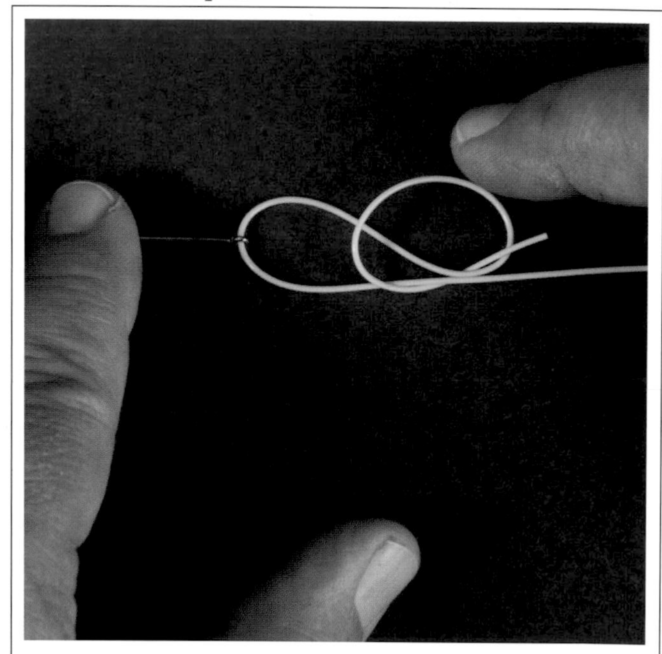

Tuck the working end around the standing part and back through the loop to form an overhand loop (see page 30).

it in the 1970s. Dunaway authored the *Complete Book of Baits, Rigs, and Tackle*, a compendium of fishing knowledge that has been a bible to many anglers for more than twenty years.

Have patience when working with smaller knots. Tying the perfect knot takes practice.

Uni-Knot: Step 3

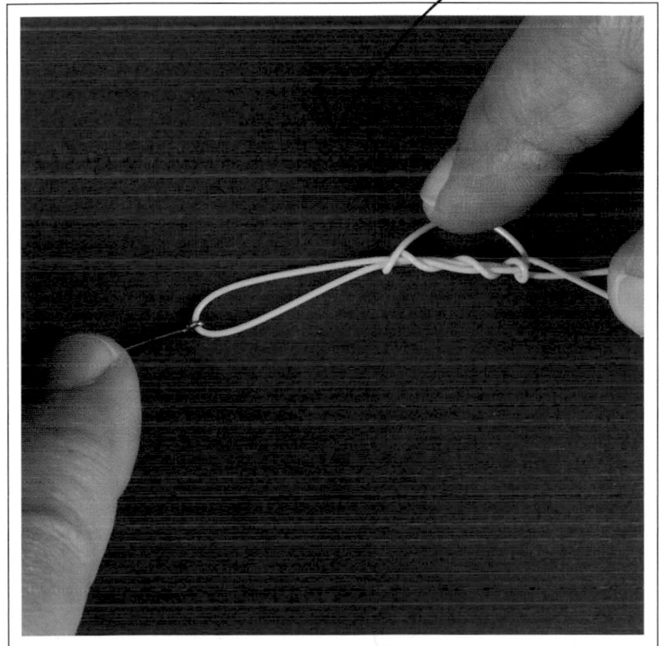

Make four or five turns of the end through the loop and around the standing part.

Uni-Knot: Step 4

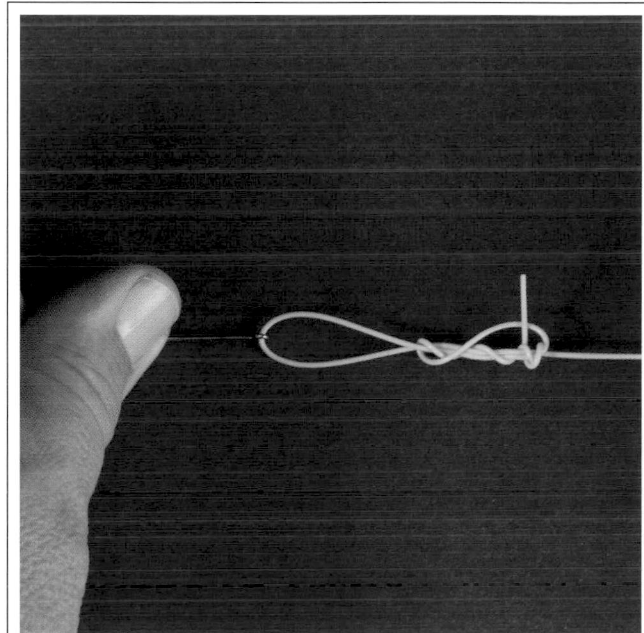

Tighten the knot by pulling on the standing part and trim off the tag end.

DOUBLE TURLE KNOT

A knot used primarily for tying a fly to a tippet.

The double Turle knot is a simple angling knot that secures the line to the shank of a fly hook (or any hook). With a single loop in the line, a Turle will be tied, and with two loops you get the double Turle, a slightly more difficult knot to tie but a more secure knot. When using a tipped eye, an eye that lies at an angle to the shank, the line draws directly from the knot without compromising any of the line's strength. Dating back at least to the early 1800s, this knot was popularized by Major William Greer Turle, who never claimed to have invented it.

Double Turle Knot: Step 1

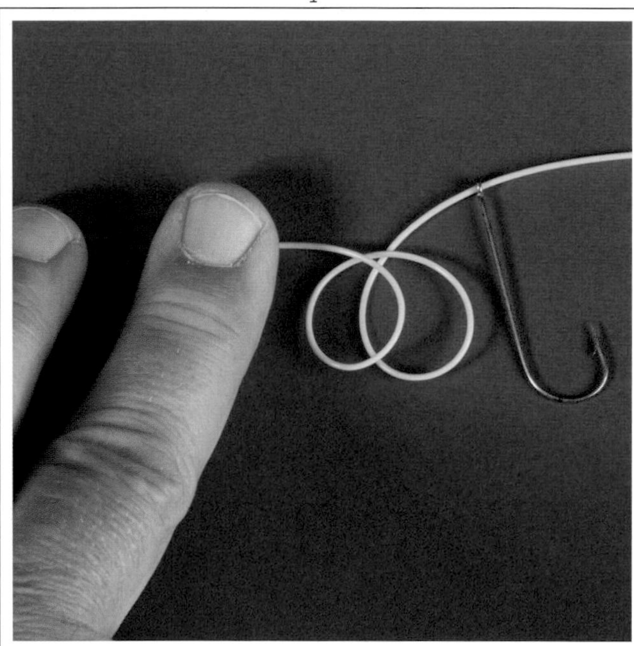

Thread the line through the eye of the hook and form two loops, one sitting on top of the other.

Double Turle Knot: Step 2

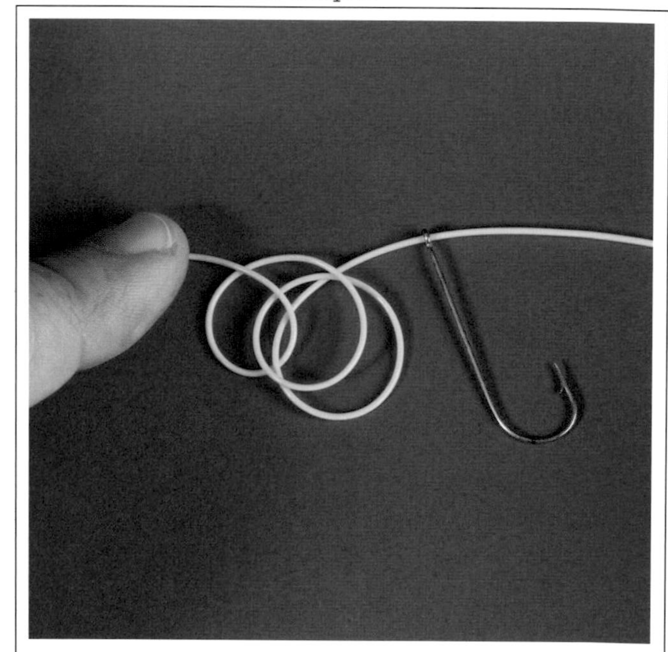

Tuck the working end through both loops, as shown in the photograph.

ZOOM

The *tag end* is the short length of the working end that extends beyond the knot after the knot is tightened. It is clipped off by fly fishermen to add more realism to the action of the fly.

Double Turle Knot: Step 3

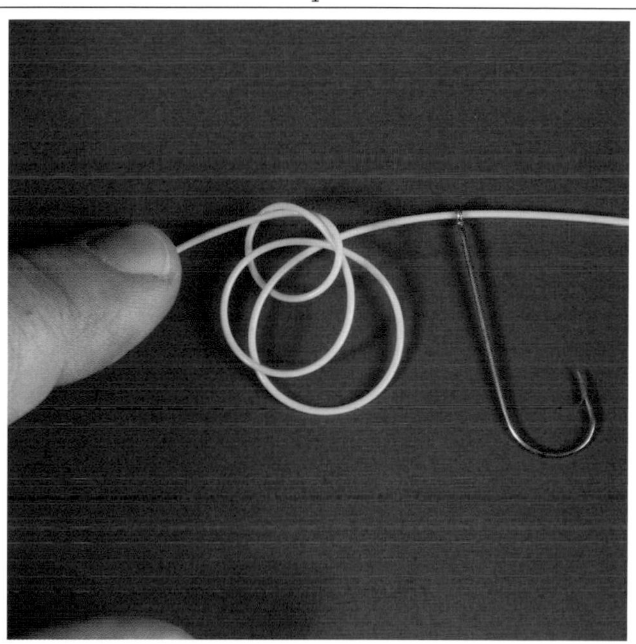

Tie the working end into an overhand knot (see page 18) that encircles both loops.

Double Turle Knot: Step 4

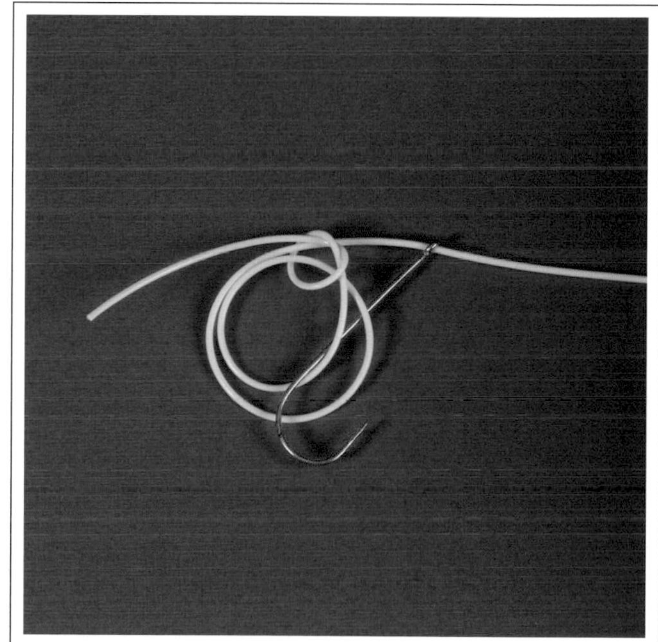

Bring the hook through both loops so the knot can be tightened against the shank. Trim off the tag end.

CRAWFORD KNOT

A fast-tying knot for changing a lure or fly in a hurry.

Although overlooked by many devout anglers, the Crawford is a versatile knot useful in attaching line to flies, hooks, swivels and lures. The Crawford has two big advangtages: The knot ties quickly and its ten *crossing points*, the places where a part of the line (or rope) overlaps another part of the line, make it hold fairly well considering its simplicity.

The X over the original loop tells that the knot is being tied correctly.

Crawford Knot: Step 1

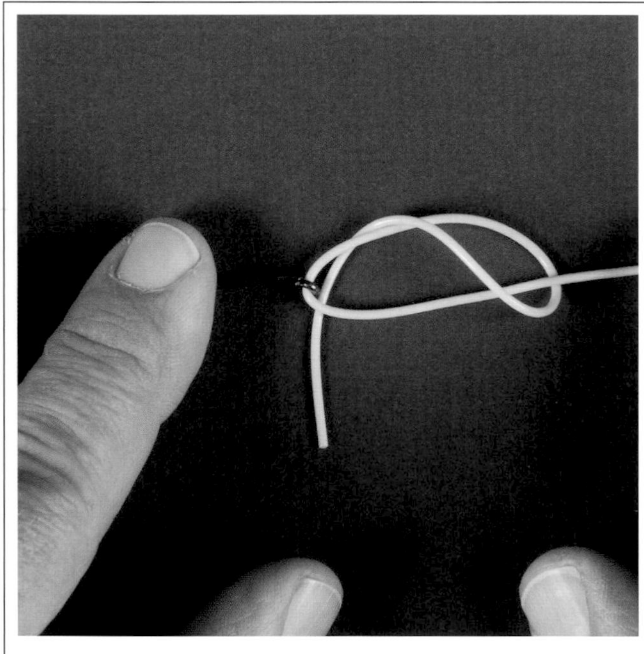

Thread the line through the eye of the hook and bring the working end around the standing part and back underneath the loop created.

Crawford Knot: Step 2

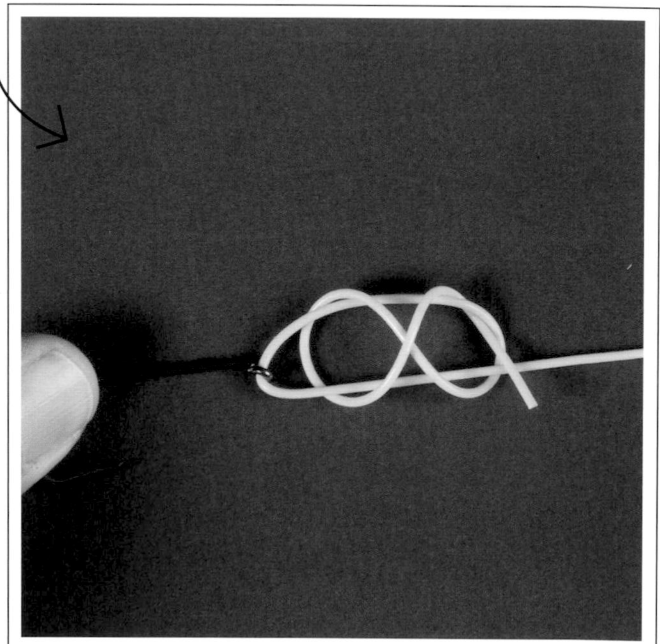

Bring the working end up over the loop and down through the newly created loop (from the back). Pull on the working end to tighten the knot, then slide the knot against the eye of the shank. Trim off the tag end.

CAIRNTON (WOODS) KNOT

A knot for tying the line to the shank of a hook.

While similar to the dry fly knot (see page 130) in function, the Cairnton knot (also known as the Woods knot) is simpler to tie. When used with an eye that is tipped at an angle to the shank of the hook, it can be situated to pull a straight line. This knot is also popular for tying a swivel to the end of a line.

Cairnton Knot: Step 1

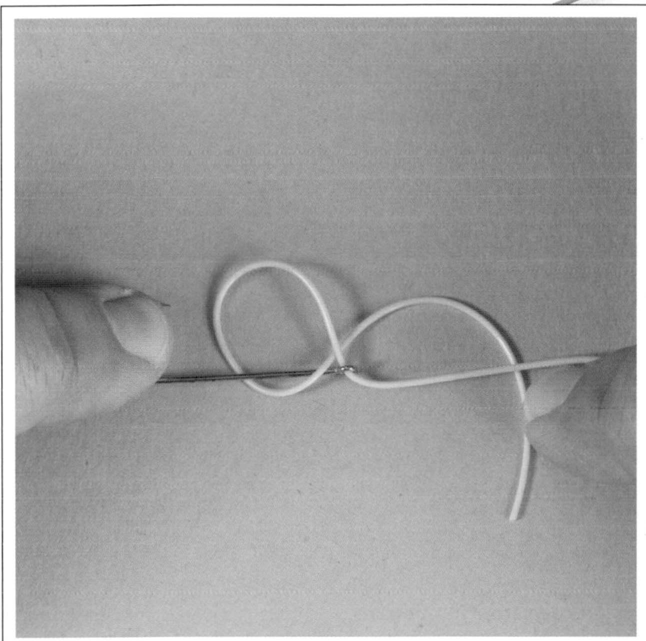

Thread the line through the eye. Loop the working end around the shank of the hook, as shown in the photograph.

GREEN LIGHT

This knot was first mentioned in *Fisherman's Knots and Wrinkles,* by W. A. Hunter

Cairnton Knot: Step 2

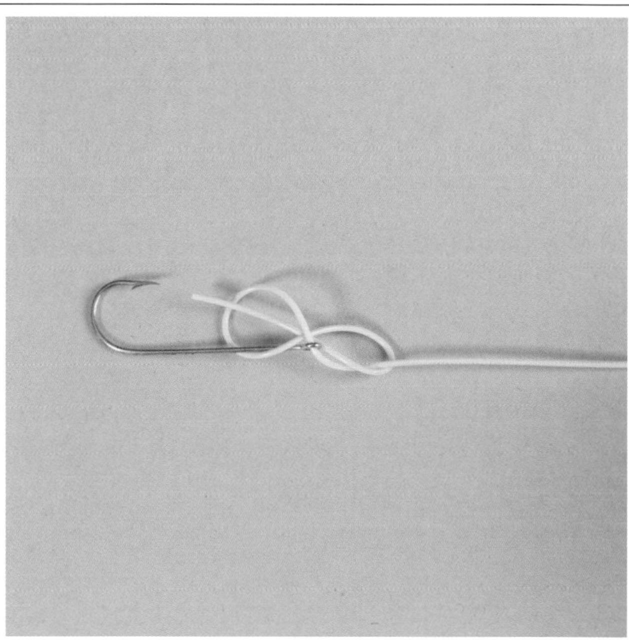

Loop the working end around the standing part and back through the first loop. Push the second loop onto the shank and snug the knot against the eye. Trim off the tag end.

TRILENE KNOT

Takes the line through the eye of the hook twice, for larger eyes.

A knot attaching line to a hook is stronger if the line passes through the eye of the hook twice. This is what the Trilene knot does. It only works, of course, when the eye is large enough for the line to fit through twice. It can be difficult to tighten in heavy lines (those made to withstand twelve or more pounds of pull) but when it tightens it can be depended upon to resist slipping. Not only for attaching larger hooks to line, this useful knot

Trilene Knot: Step 1

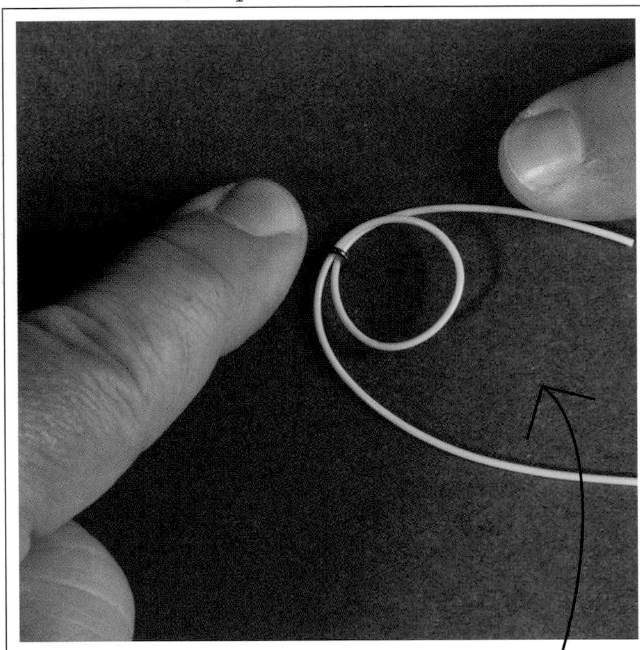

Thread the line through the eye twice.

Be sure the eye of the hook is large enough for the line to fit through twice.

Trilene Knot: Step 2

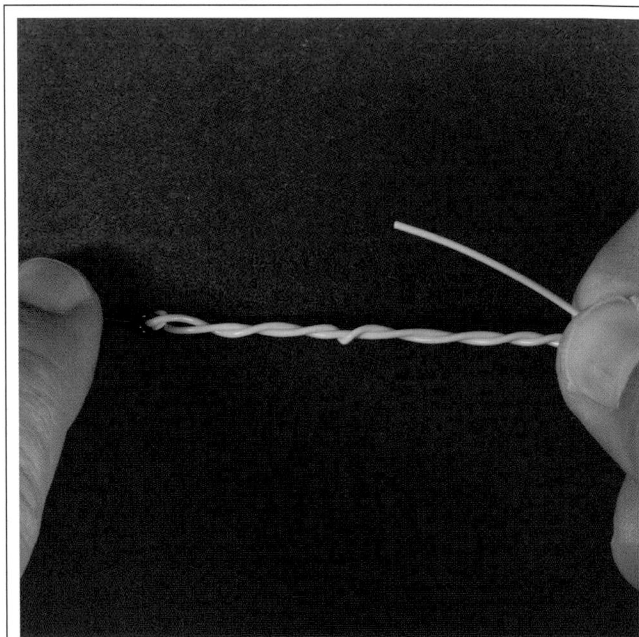

Twist the working end four or five times around the standing part.

works for attaching swivels, snaps, and artificial lures. Trilene is a brand of monofilament developed by the Berkley company, one of the world's largest manufacturers of fishing equipment, and the name implies that this knot was developed for that line.

ZOOM

Monofilament fishing line is made from a single long, thin polymer fiber. The fiber is produced in varying thicknesses, so the line is available in many strengths..

Trilene Knot: Step 3

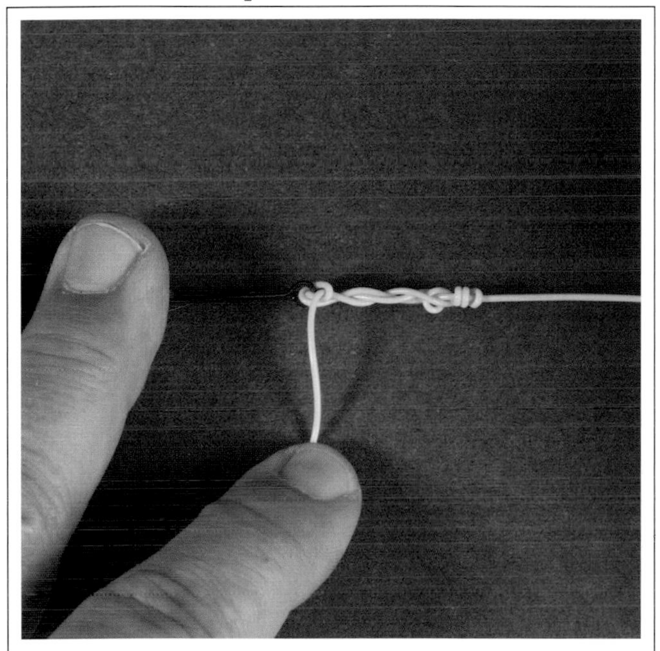

Bring the working end back through the round turn of the line at the eye.

Trilene Knot: Step 4

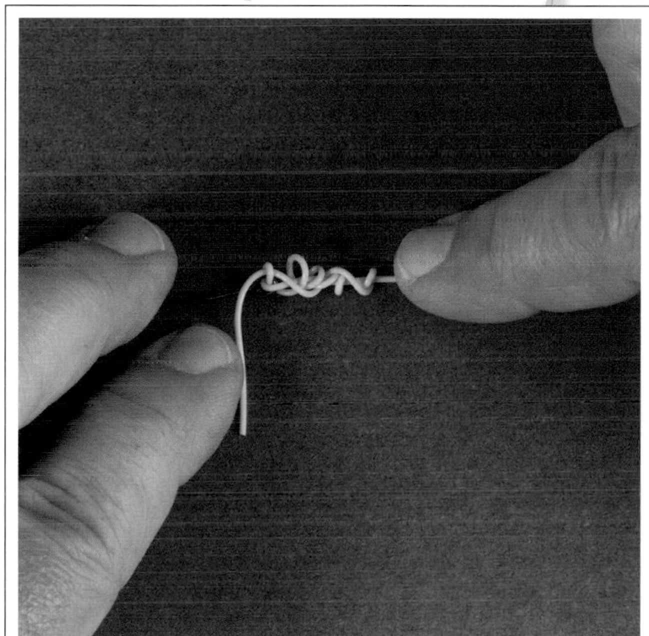

Pull the working end and push the knot against the eye before tugging on the standing part for the final tightening. Trim off the tag end.

SIMPLE SNELL

A simple variation of snelling, used primarily in saltwater fishing.

Snelling is most often thought of as a method of tying a heavy line to a large hook, and it is popular with anglers who seek large saltwater species such as tuna, marlin, salmon, and dolphin. It can, however, be used on any size hook—and often is, as long as the hook has an eye.

Snelling creates a strong connection between the line and the shank of the hook—instead of tying the line directly to the eye—and therefore reduces the strength of

Simple Snell: Step 1

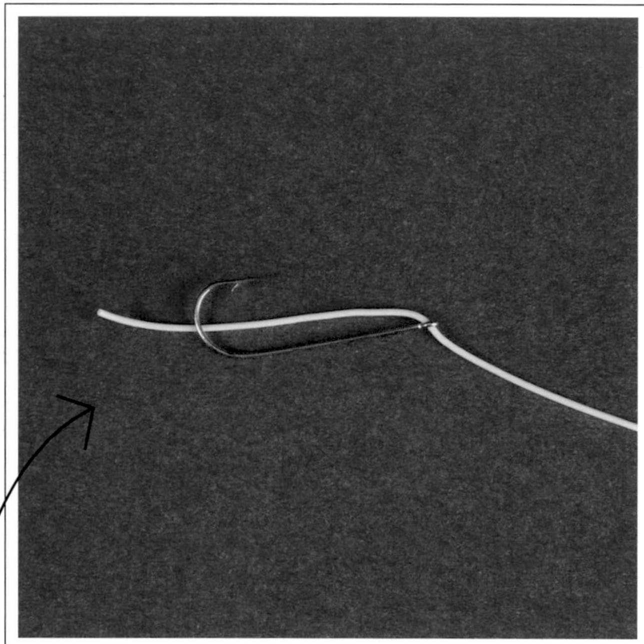

Thread the line through the eye of the hook and lay it along the shank of the hook.

Be sure to pull enough line through the eye to make four or five wraps around the shank.

Simple Snell: Step 2

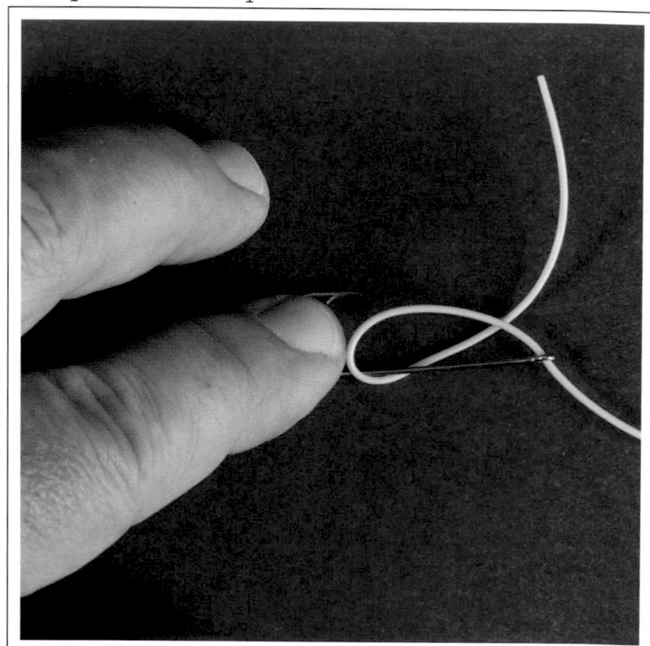

Loop the line back along the shank, and hold the loop against the shank.

the line very little. The simple snell is quicker and easier than the full version of snelling (see page 142), but it is slightly weaker and less secure. This knot is used only for fishing.

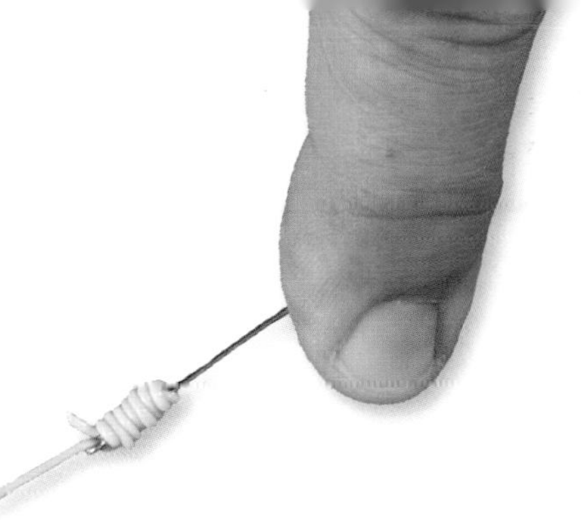

Simple Snell: Step 3

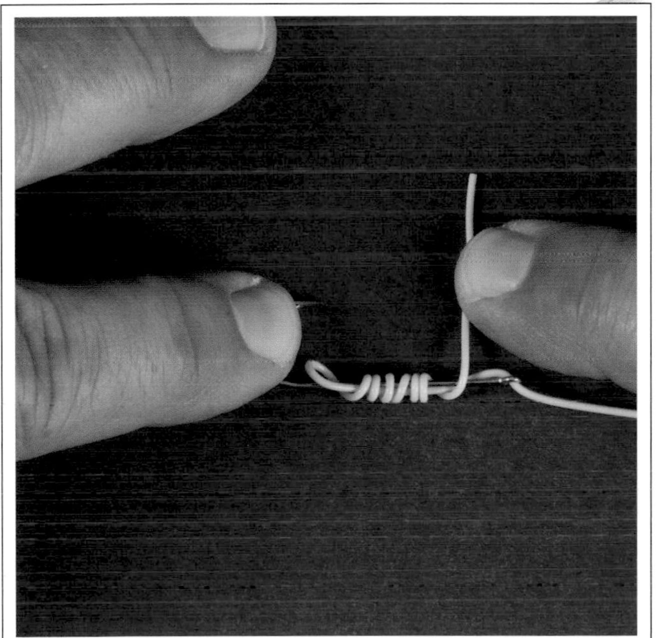

Wrap the line four or five times around the shank (and itself), moving back toward the eye.

Simple Snell: Step 4

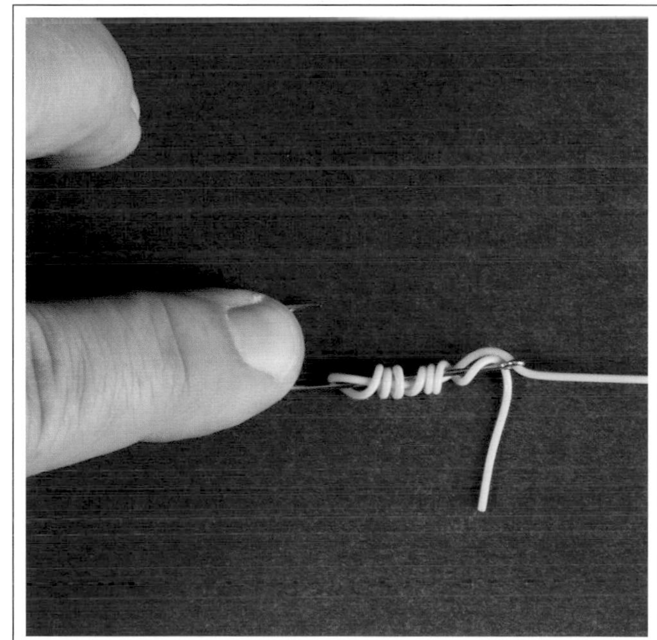

Tuck the working end down between the shank and the line, and tighten by pulling on the standing part.

SNELLING A HOOK

An extremely secure knot for heavy hooks, used primarily in saltwater fishing.

This knot ties a line to the shank of a hook with extreme security. The word *snelling* arose in the deep-sea fishing industry. It was used by long-liners, who anchor numerous large hooks to a long line, before being adopted by saltwater sport fishermen.

Be sure to pull enough line through the eye to make at least four or five wraps.

Snelling a Hook: Step 1

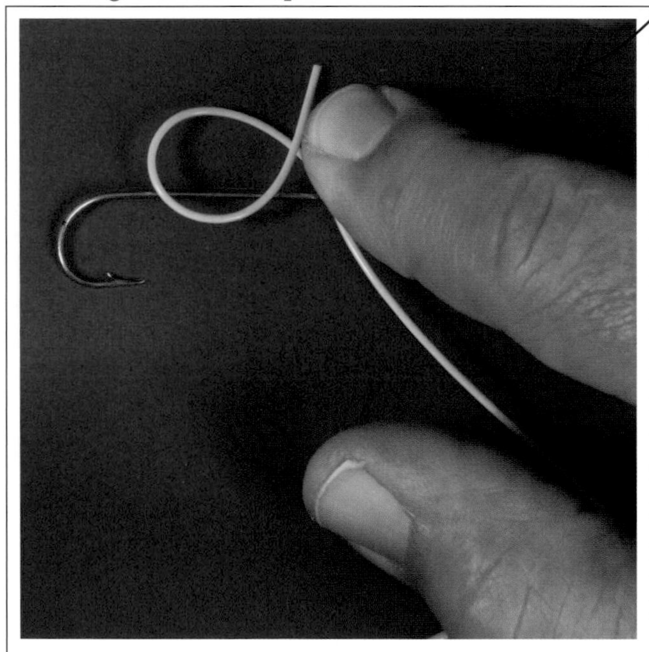

Thread the line through the eye of the hook and form a fairly large loop back toward the eye, as shown in the photograph.

Snelling a Hook: Step 2

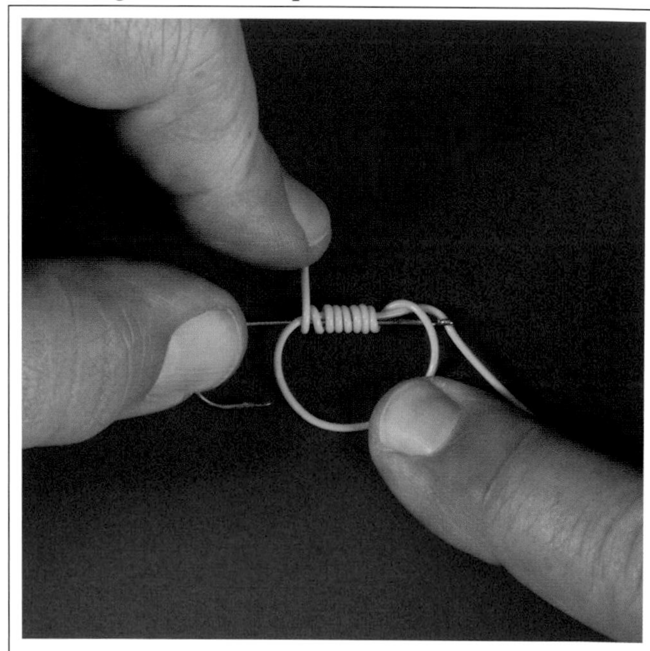

Lay the standing part along the shank and wrap the working end around the line and shank *within the loop,* moving toward the hook. Make four or five wraps—or more—then tighten.

TANDEM HOOK KNOT

A knot used for attaching a second hook to a line in tandem with the first hook.

A second hook can be attached higher up on a line before attaching a hook to the end of the line. This is especially useful in saltwater fishing and allows a large bait fish to be attached twice, one hook in the head and the second near the tail. This is a simple and secure knot.

Be sure to pull enough line through the eye to allow a hook to be tied to the end.

Tandem Hook Knot: Step 1

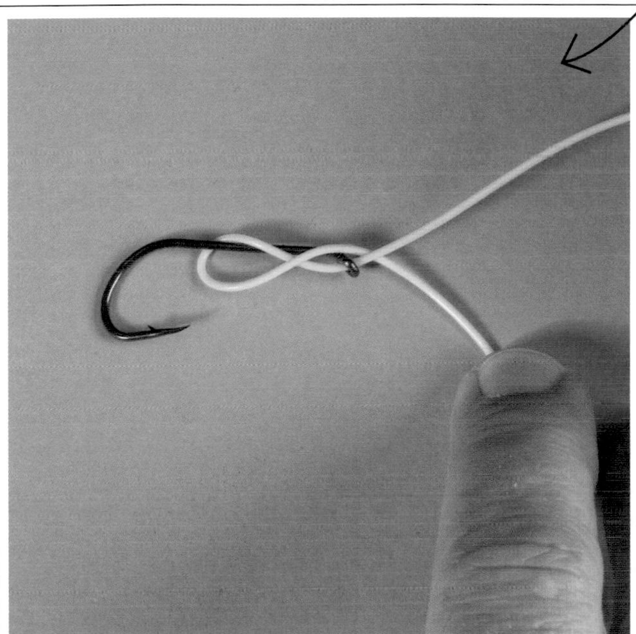

Thread the line through the eye of the hook and loop the line around the shank of the hook.

Tandem Hook Knot: Step 2

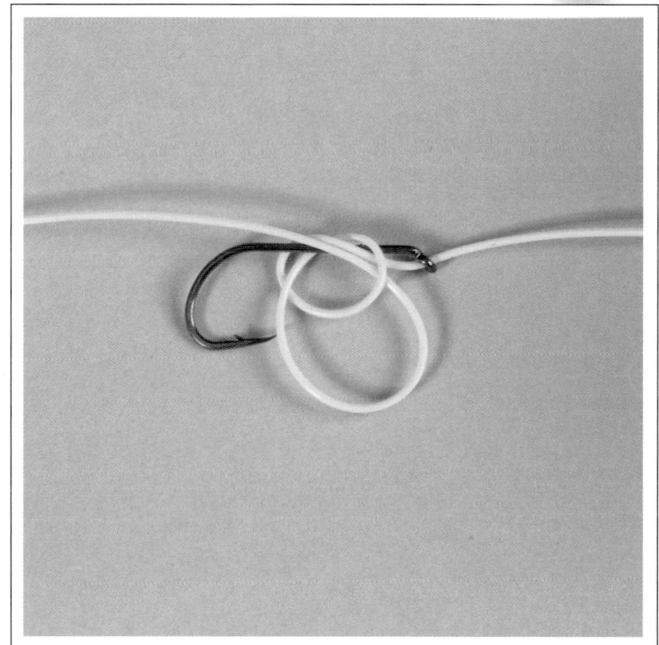

Tie an overhand knot (see page 18) around the shank and bring the working end through the overhand a second time, forming essentially a double overhand around the shank. Tighten.

SWIVEL KNOT

A knot used for attaching a swivel to a line.

A fishing lure, as the name implies, is anything tied to a fishing line to lure a fish into biting. If a lure is tied directly to the end of a line, it tends to move unrealistically through the water. Thus the swivel. The swivel is attached directly to the line, and the lure is attached to the swivel.

The swivel turns freely at the end of the line, allowing the lure to move much more realistically. Swivels also allow quick and easy changing of lures since no tying is required to make a switch. They are used in fresh- and saltwater fishing.

Swivel Knot: Step 1

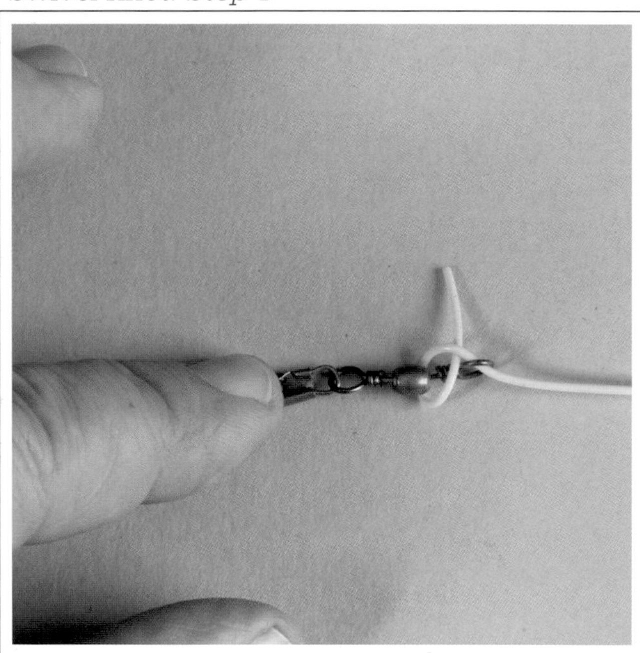

Thread the line through the ring of the swivel and loop it around the neck of the swivel, as shown in the photograph.

Swivel Knot: Step 2

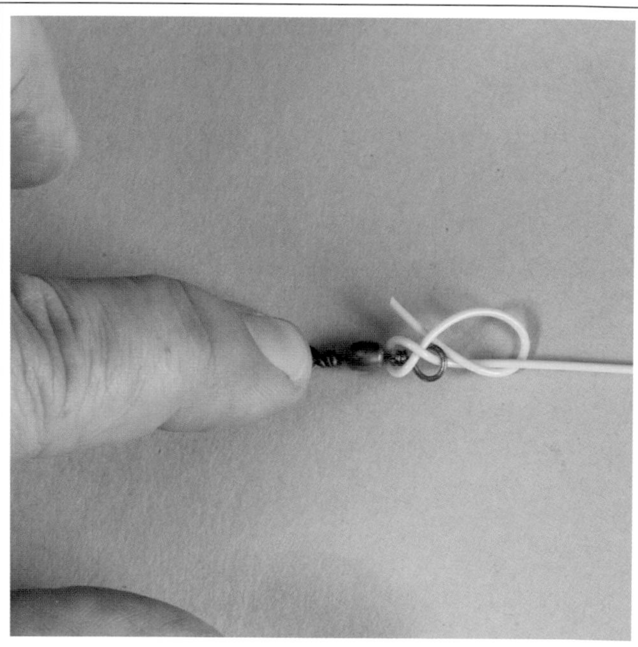

Loop the working end around the standing part, as shown in the photograph.

GREEN LIGHT

This knot can be used in camping to keep a sack closed.

This quick and easy knot, used to attach a swivel to a fishing line, is not as secure as more intricate knots, but for lighter lines and smaller species it works well. In the years before prepackaged foods, a similarly tied knot was used to hold the mouth of a sack closed—and was called, appropriately, the sack-binding knot or bag-binding knot. The swivel knot has been listed in knot books dating back more than fifty years.

Swivel Knot: Step 3

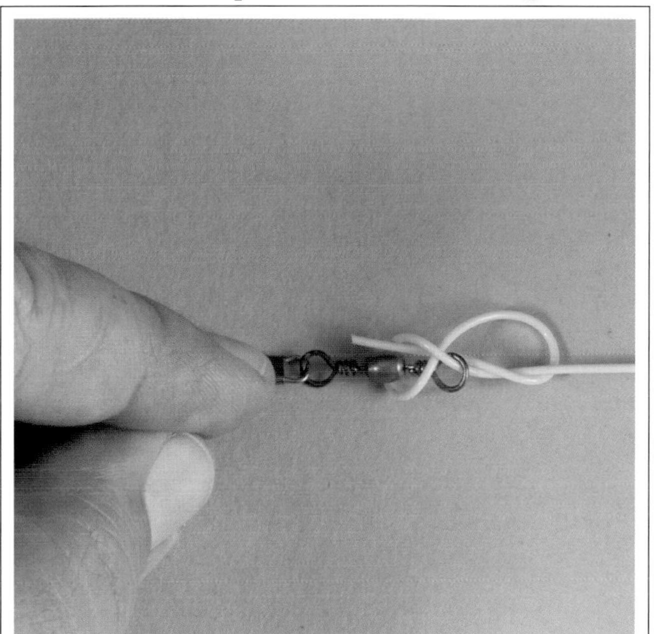

Bring the working end through the loop that was formed around the neck of the swivel.

RED LIGHT

Since monofilament fishing line doesn't float and is virtually invisible in water, it might entangle fish and mammals if cut and left to sink.

Swivel Knot: Step 4

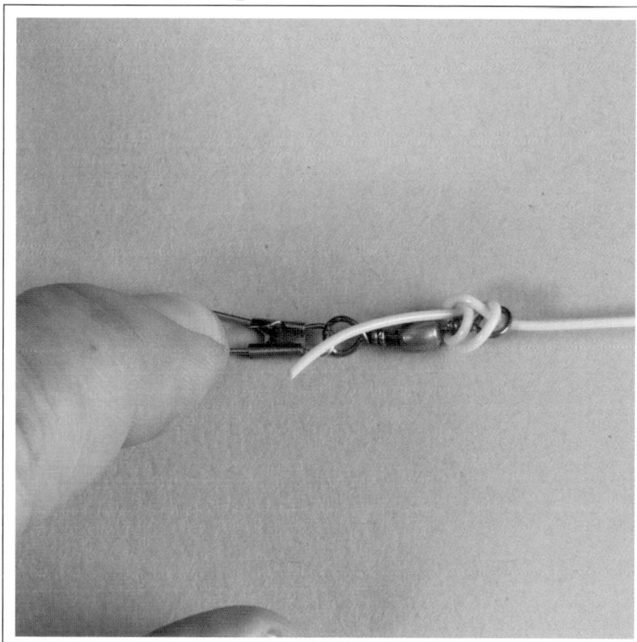

Push the loop above the swivel onto the neck and tighten the knot around the neck.

PALOMAR KNOT

A knot used for attaching a swivel, lure, or hook to a line.

More secure than the swivel knot (see page 144), the Palomar knot is a very easy knot to learn. After a bit of practice, it can be tied with very little light for illumination. The Palomar requires the swivel, hook, or lure to be passed through the knot before completion and therefore might be difficult to tie in lines with multiple hooks or another complicated arrangement of tackle. It ties in a bight, which shortens the line a bit more than other knots.

The Palomar knot is recommended by the International Game Fish Association as the strongest of all fish-

Palomar Knot: Step 1

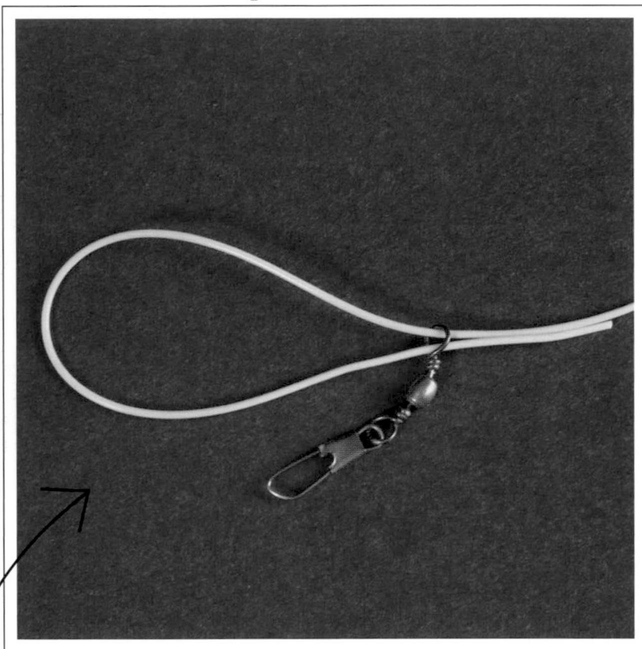

Thread a bight of line through the ring or eye of the hook as shown in the photo.

Be sure the bight is long enough to tie the rest of the knot.

Palomar Knot: Step 2

Bring the bight and the swivel, lure, or hook back alongside the standing part.

ing knots. The name *Palomar* suggests that this knot is related, somehow, to Mount Palomar in California, but the significance of the name remains unclear. This knot is used only for fishing.

Palomar Knot: Step 3

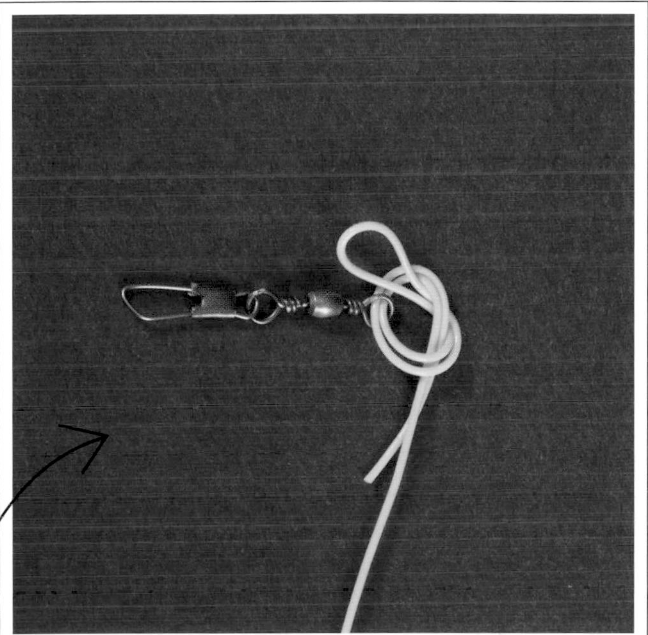

Tie an overhand knot (see page 18) in the bight.

This bight will shorten the line.

Palomar Knot: Step 4

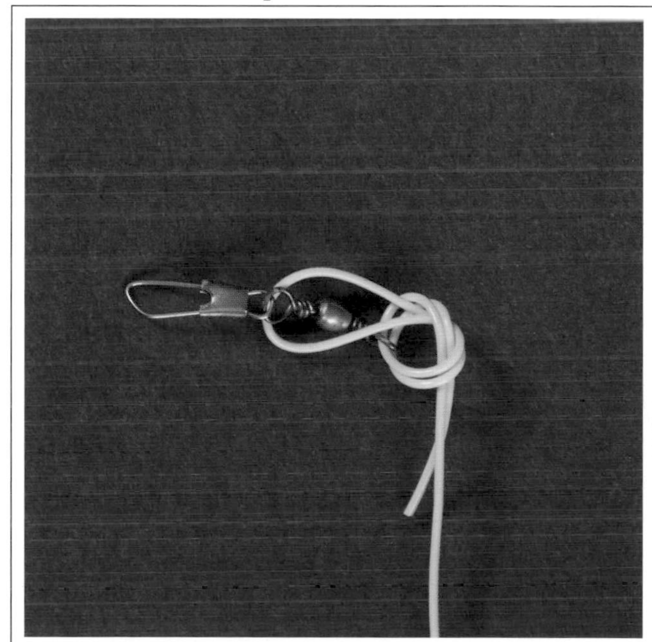

Pull the swivel, lure, or hook out through the bight and tighten the knot.

WORLD'S FAIR KNOT

A knot used for attaching a swivel, lure, or hook to the line.

The world's fair knot secures a swivel, lure, or hook to the line with a bight but without passing the tackle through the knot. It is easier, therefore, to tie onto complicated tackle arrangements than the Palomar knot (see page 146). It is a secure knot, resisting slippage (and the loss of a fish).

ZOOM

This knot, created by Gary Martin, won a new fishing line competition at the 1982 World's Fair.

World's Fair Knot: Step 1

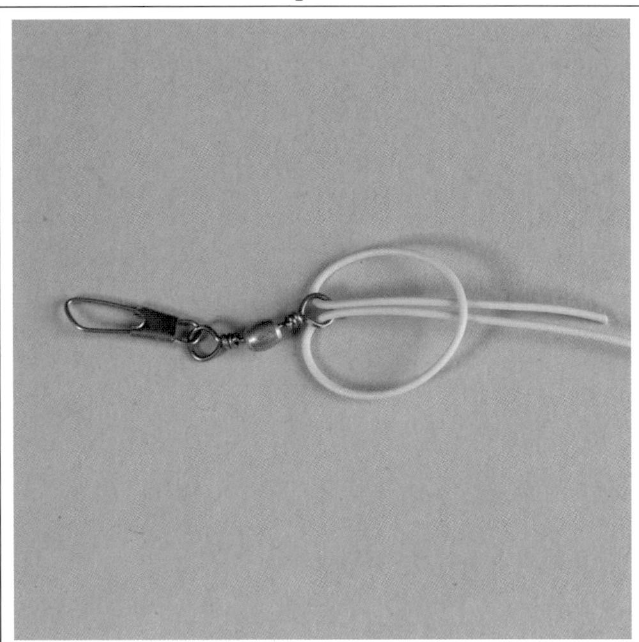

Thread a bight of line through the ring or eye of the hook and double it over to lie on both standing parts, as shown in the photograph.

World's Fair Knot: Step 2

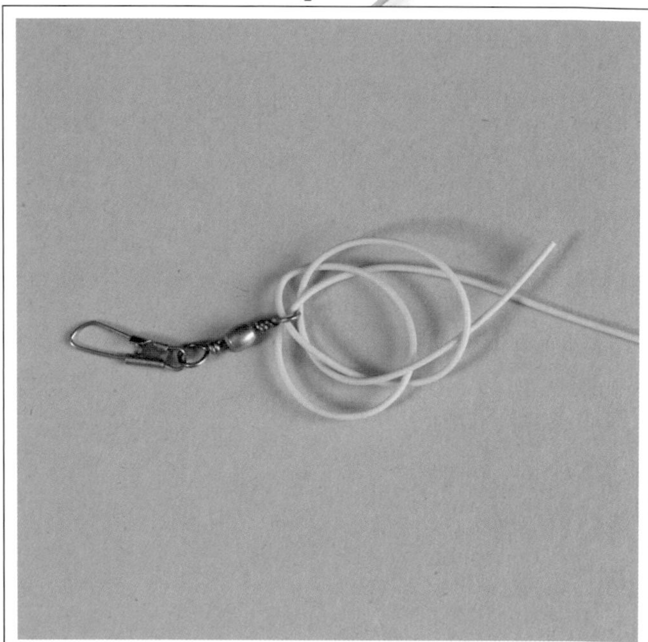

Tuck the working end through both loops, going underneath the two standing parts, then bring the working end through the new loop created in the standing part. Align the knot by pulling on the standing part and working end simultaneously. Last, tighten the knot.

INTERLOCKING LOOPS

A knot used to join two lines with loops tied in the working ends.

Interlocking loops can be tied in any material and any size line. They remove the strain on the actual knots that form the loops and create a strong connection between two lines. The loops must be interlocked correctly or one line will cut through the other. The loops must interlock to form a square knot, not a girth hitch.

Notice the square knot configuration.

Interlocking Loops: Step 1

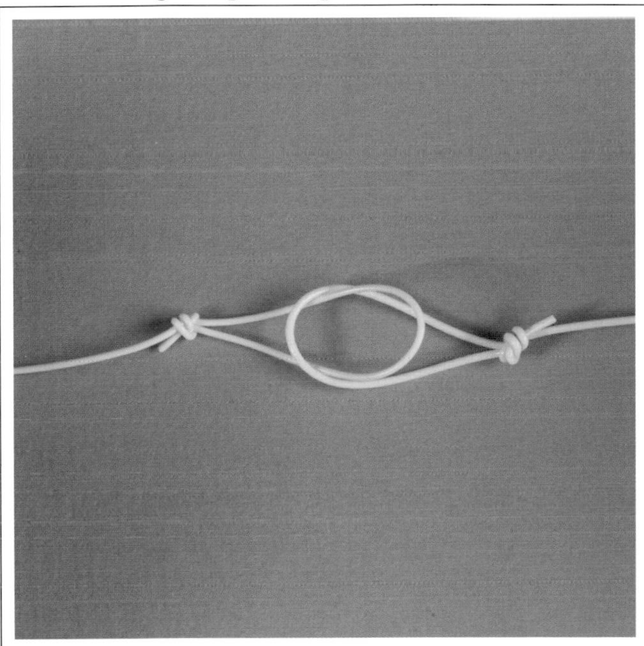

Tie a loop in the working end of both lines. (Many knots will work to create the loops. An overhand on a bight is used in the photographs.) Lay one loop inside the other, as shown in the photograph.

Interlocking Loops: Step 2

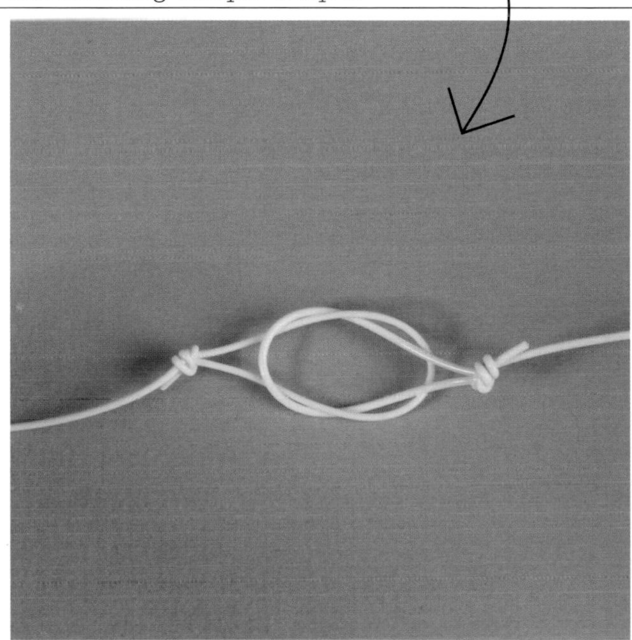

Bring the knot of the outer loop, and the rest of that line, through the inner loop.

GREEN LIGHT

This knot may be used in camping and boating.

BLOOD KNOT

A knot used for joining two lines of the same diameter.

When two lines are approximately the same diameter, especially monofilament, the blood knot serves to join them in a fairly strong connection. It is sometimes called the barrel knot, referring to the fact that the tightened knot takes on a barrel shape. It can be used on lines of differing diameter, but the thinner line should be doubled for more security.

Several variations of the knot exist. They entail wrapping the lines around each other from the outside toward the center instead of wrapping them around each

Blood Knot: Step 1

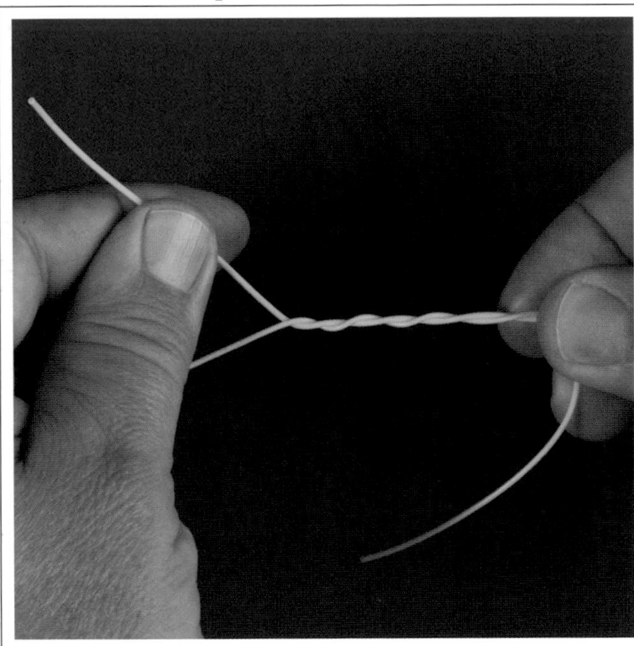

Lay the working ends of the two lines alongside each other and make five to seven turns of one line around the other.

Blood Knot: Step 2

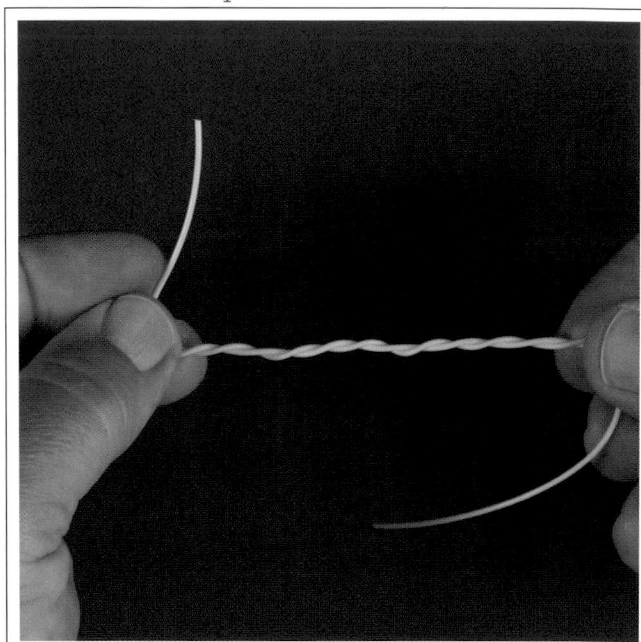

Holding the lines and turns in position, make an equal number of turns of the second line around the first.

other from the center toward the outside of the knot. The method shown here is the preferred version.

Whether tied from inside out or outside in, the number of coils in the knot should be the same in both lines to ensure maximum security. The blood knot is used by some fly fishermen to tie the leader to the fly fishing line.

Take care to tuck the second working end through the gap in the opposite direction of the first working end.

Blood Knot: Step 3

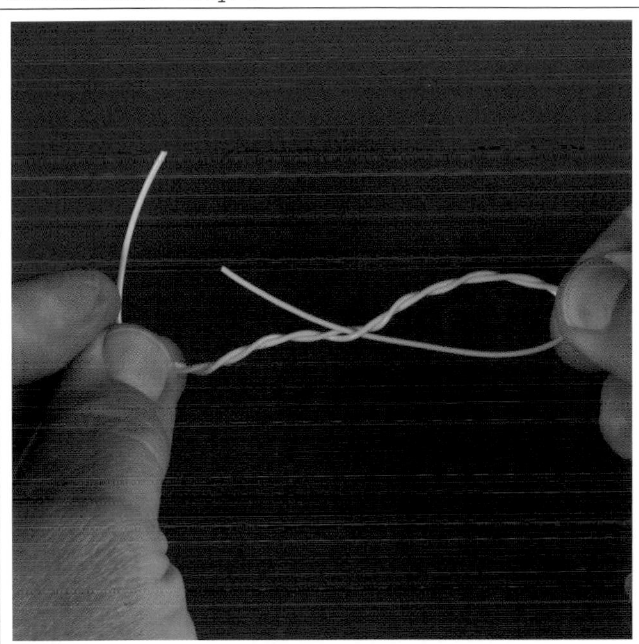

Take the working end of one line through the gap between the two sets of turns.

Blood Knot: Step 4

Take the working end of the second line through the gap between the two sets of turns, and tighten.

ALBRIGHT KNOT

Used for joining two lines, especially if they are of different diameters.

Two lines can be joined securely with the Albright knot, a fairly simple knot to learn. This knot works especially well if the two lines are of different diameters, making it popular for attaching a leader to fly fishing line. It works if the lines are of different materials as well, such as joining monofilament to braid or braid to wire. The coils of the line being wrapped (the smaller line) should lie neatly beside each other, not overlying each other. For more security, some anglers coat the finished knot with rubber cement or tie a backup knot in the working end of the lighter line.

Albright Knot: Step 1

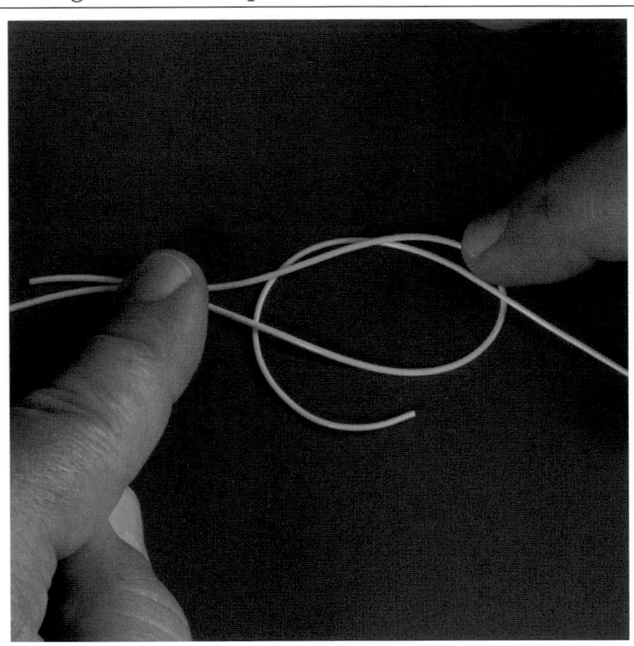

Form a bight in the working end of one of the lines. If the lines are of different sizes, make the bight in the larger line. Take the working end of the second line through the bight and back underneath the bight, as shown in the photograph.

Albright Knot: Step 2

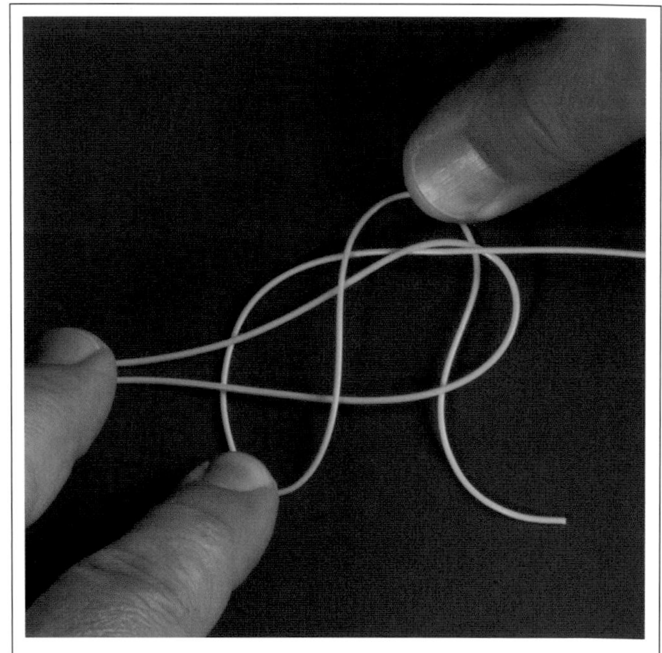

Bring the working end up and over the bight to create the first turn.

As a simple backup knot, wrap the working end around the standing part of the lighter line three times, wrapping the line toward the Albright, not away from it. This backup knot is essentially one half of a blood knot (see page 150). When tied neatly, and with the tag ends trimmed off, the Albright knot passes through the eyes of most fishing rods without catching.

Take care to tuck the second working end through the gap in the opposite direction of the first working end.

Albright Knot: Step 3

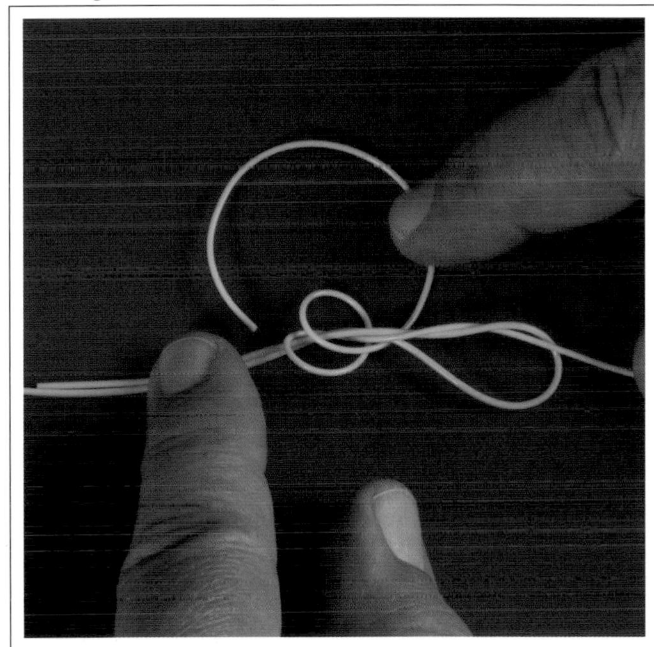

Continue to make turns around all three strands, working toward the end of the bight, the number of turns increasing if the diameter of the line is small.

Albright Knot: Step 4

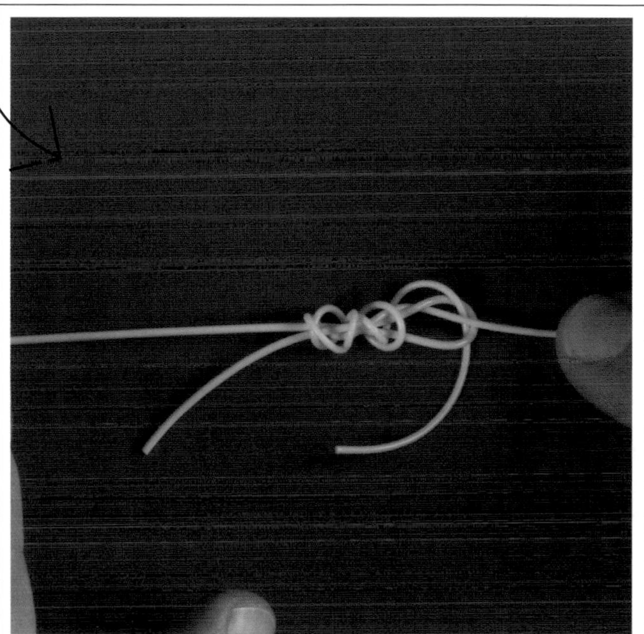

Take the working end out through the loop and tighten the knot.

DOUBLE UNI-KNOT

A knot that joins two lines with identical knots tied back to back.

The double universal knot, or double uni-knot for short, is two universal knots, or uni-knots (see page 132), tied back to back, one in each line. You get a very secure connection between the two lines when the knots are tightened to jam against each other.

The double uni-knot, also known as the double grinner knot, ties quickly after a little practice. Serving the same purpose as the blood knot, it is easier to tie than the blood knot. It does not diminish the strength of the line, even when a sudden jerk is applied (the kind of jerk

Double Uni-Knot: Step 1

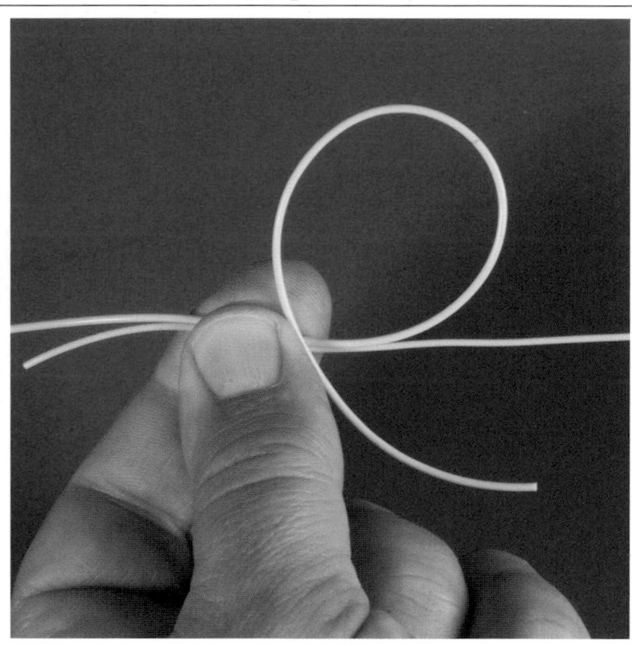

Hold the two lines together and form a loop in one line, as shown in the photograph.

Double Uni-Knot: Step 2

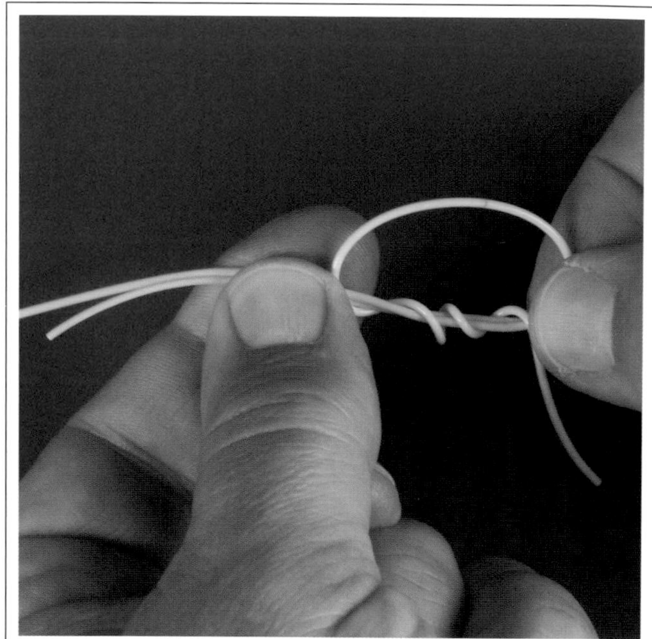

Make five or more turns of the line around both lines within the loop.

all anglers long for, indicating that a big fish has hit).

If the species of fish being sought is very large, such as a monster of the deep blue sea, the double uni's security can be increased by tying the knot in lines that are first doubled over into large bights. This knot is not used in line other than fishing line because it creates a bulky and unwieldy lump of rope or cord.

ZOOM

Fishing expert and prolific writer Vic Dunaway, who is credited with inventing the universal knot, claims it is "the only knot you need to know."

Double Uni-Knot: Step 3

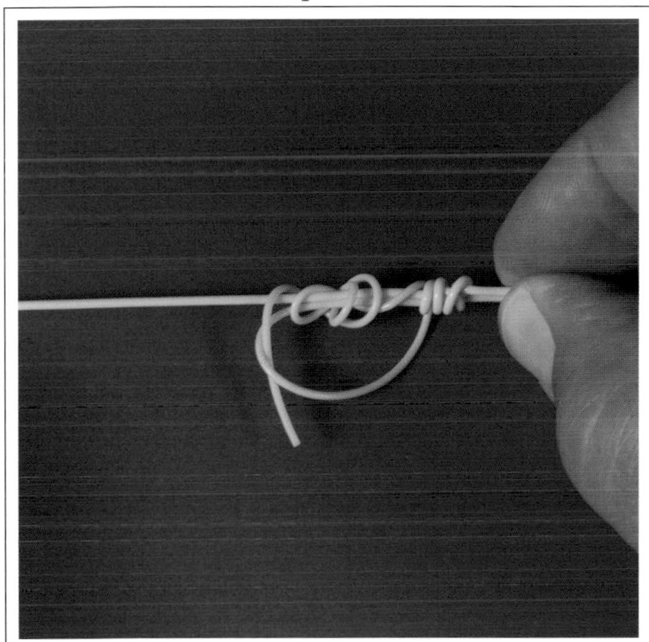

Tighten this first uni-knot against the second line.

Double Uni-Knot: Step 4

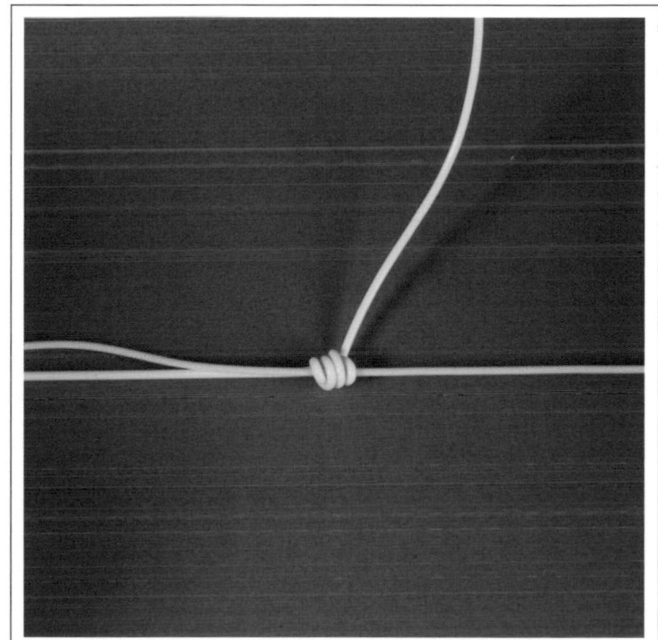

Reverse the lines in your hand. With the second line, tie a second uni-knot identical to the first but the mirror image of the first, and pull the both knots tight against each other. Trim off the tag ends.

ANGLER'S (PERFECTION) LOOP

A loop for attaching line to lure, hook, or swivel.

Sometimes called the perfection loop because it works so well for so many fishing uses in just about any type of line, the angler's loop is simple to tie and holds strong. There is more than one way to tie the angler's loop. It can, for instance, be tied as a loop separate from tackle. The entire loop can then be threaded through the ring of a small lure or swivel, the small lure or swivel passed through the loop, and the loop then tightened as with

Angler's (Perfection) Loop: Step 1

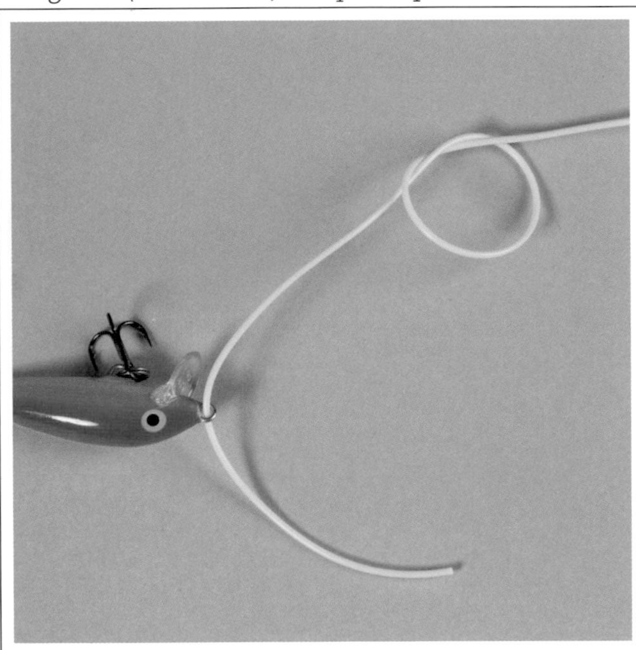

Tie an overhand knot (see page 18) several inches above the working end. Thread the working end through the eye of the hook.

Angler's (Perfection) Loop: Step 2

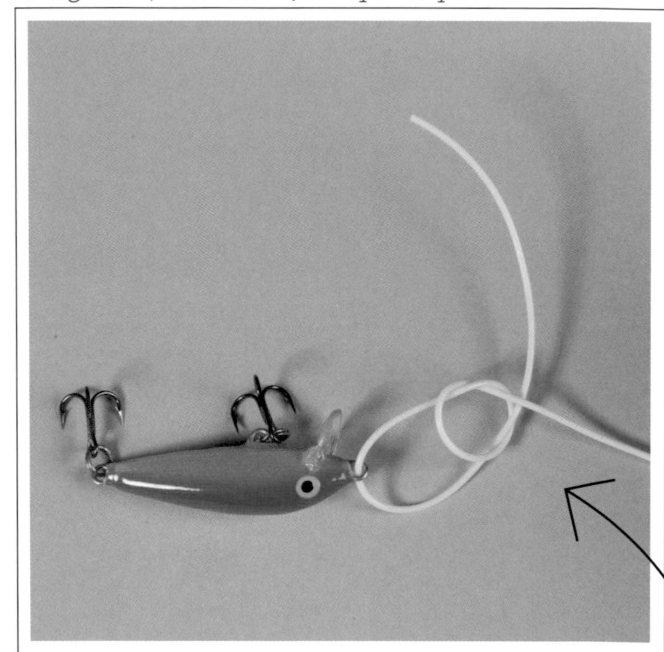

Bring the working end through the overhand knot.

While there is more than one way to tie this knot, this way works in all circumstances.

a girth hitch (see page 98). But the way shown below works in all circumstances. The knot can be used in rope or cord when a fixed loop is needed, making it useful to campers and boaters.

ZOOM

The angler's loop was used as far back as the seventeenth century, tied in lines of gut, horsehair, and silk. It is useful when tied in modern lines, and even holds in bungee cord.

Angler's (Perfection) Loop: Step 3

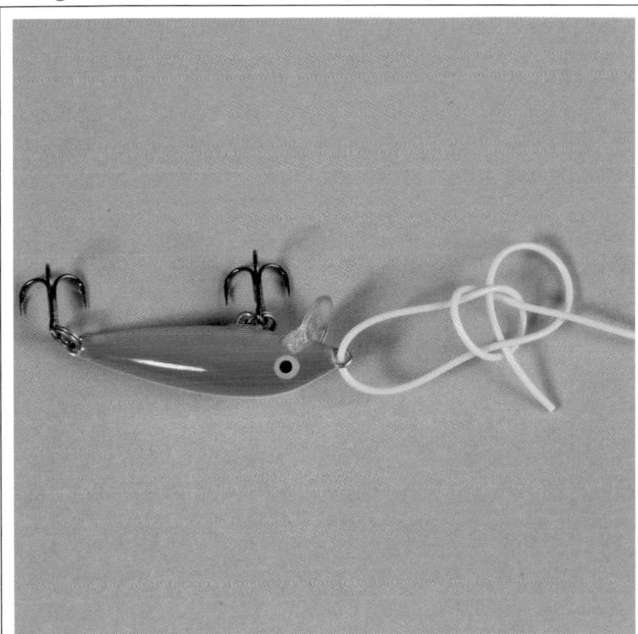

Take the working end around the standing part and back through the overhand, as shown in the photograph.

Angler's (Perfection) Loop: Step 4

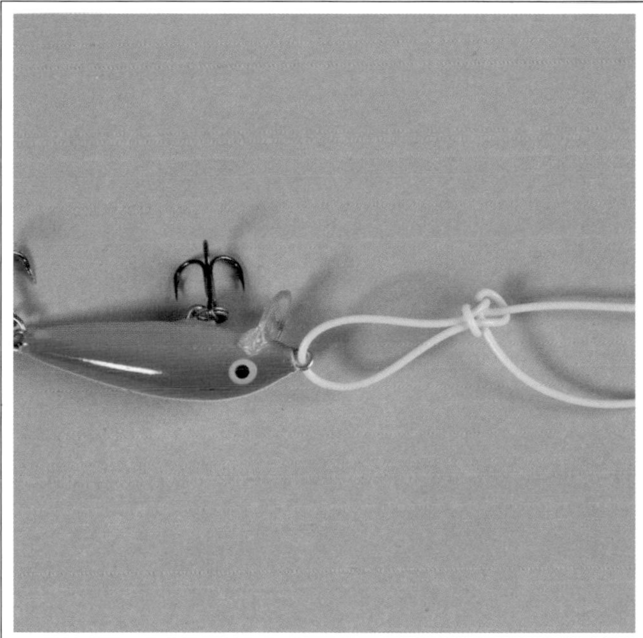

Tighten by pulling on the loop and the standing part. Trim off the tag end.

TROMBONE LOOP

An alternative fixed loop for fishing line.

In lines—or conditions, such as cold temperatures—that prove to be a problem when tying other fixed loops, or when more complicated loops have simply been forgotten, the trombone loop, tied in a bight, is a simple and easier alternative. It tends to stay fixed in the mind once learned.

Due to the abrupt angle created by the final tuck, however, this knot does weaken the line more than other

Trombone Loop: Step 1

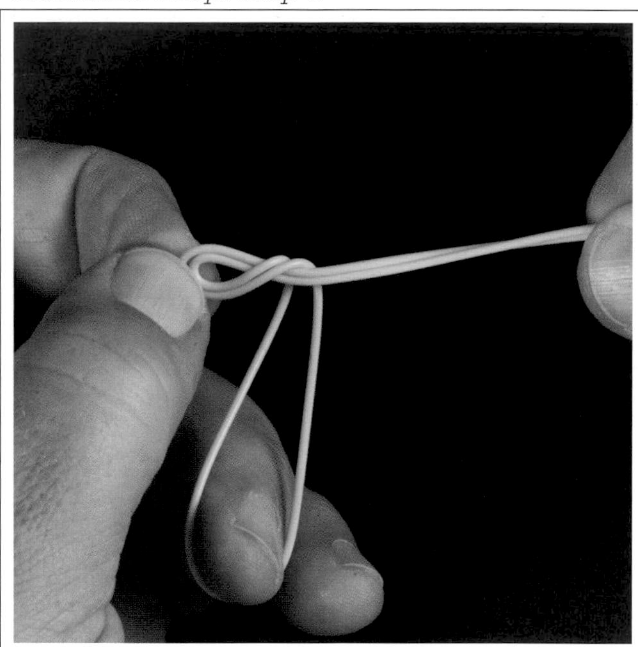

Create a bight in the line, then form a doubled loop, as shown in the photograph.

Trombone Loop: Step 2

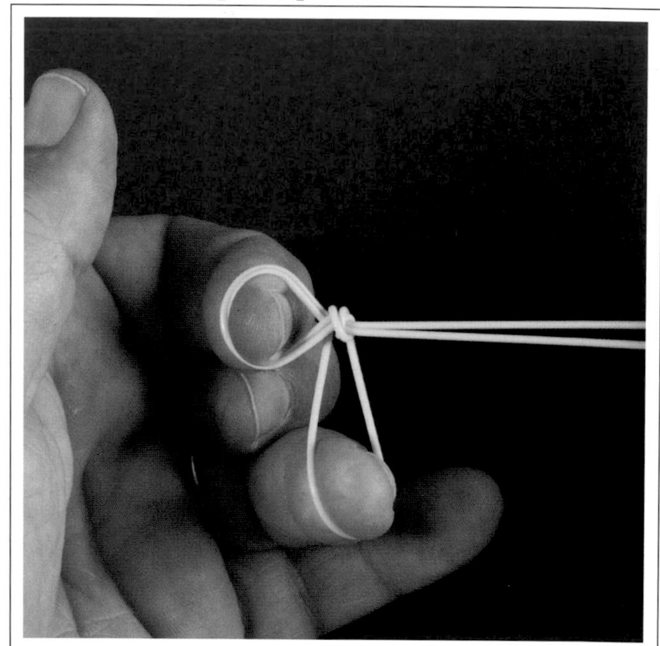

Wrap the bight around the doubled loop, moving back toward the end of the doubled loop.

loops. It should be avoided when the catch of the day could be a whopper. This loop could be tied in twine or cord and find use in camping and climbing, but it is a knot employed primarily in fishing. The name *trombone* refers to the long bight that slides into the knot during the final tightening, sort of like a trombone.

Trombone Loop: Step 3

Wrap the bight two or three times around the doubled loop and bring the end of the bight through the doubled loop.

Trombone Loop: Step 4

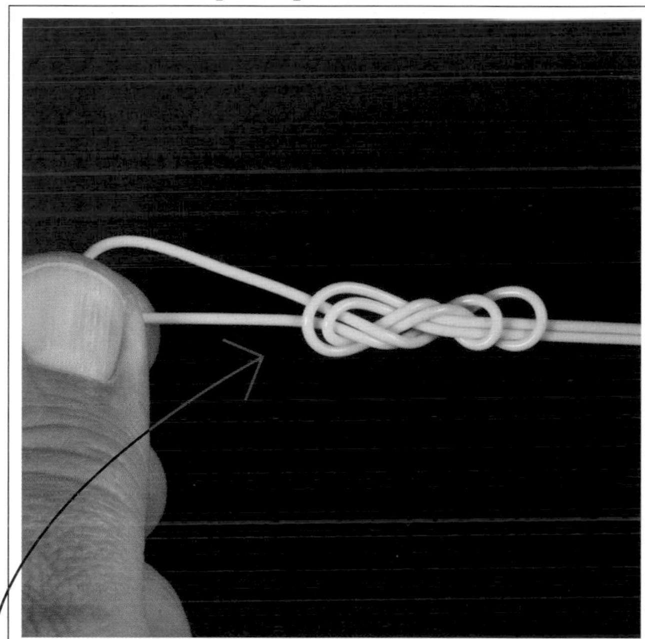

Trap the bight in the doubled loop by pulling on the standing part.

Ensure that the doubled wraps do not overlay each other but lie neatly beside each other.

RAPALA KNOT

A small, fixed loop that allows a plug to move realistically.

The Rapala knot gives a plug the freedom to jiggle about realistically on the end of the line, making the lure more tempting to a hungry fish. This knot was promoted specifically for their plugs by the Rapala company, one of the world's largest entities devoted to designing and manu-

At this point the loop can be adjusted to the required size, not too big but not tight against the ring of the lure.

Rapala Knot: Step 1

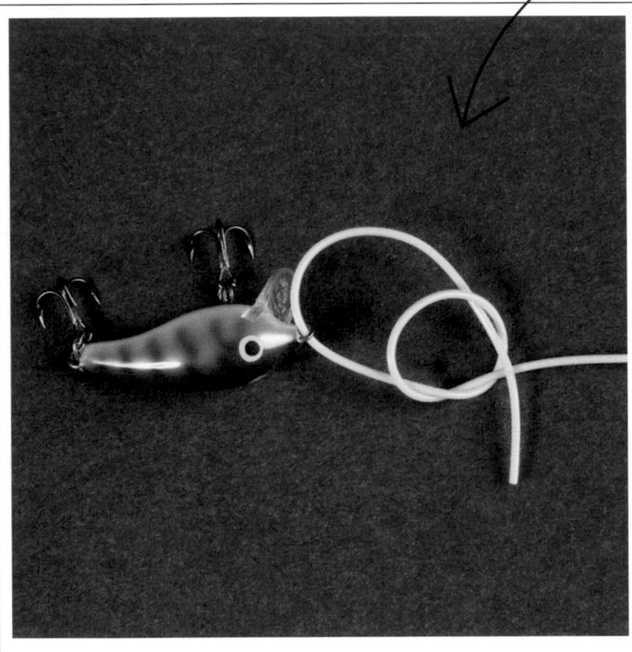

Tie an overhand knot (see page 18) several inches from the working end. Thread the working end through the eye of the plug and back through the overhand knot.

Rapala Knot: Step 2

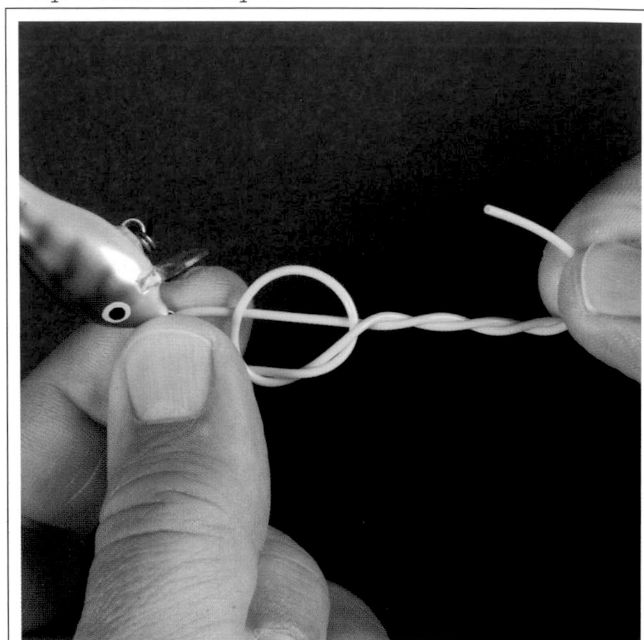

Wrap the working end a couple of times around the standing part.

facturing artificial fishing lures, but it will work on any lure or fly that needs to move about in ways that attract fish. Despite the name, the Rapala company does not claim to have invented this knot. Its origin is unknown. This is a knot used only in fishing.

Rapala Knot: Step 3

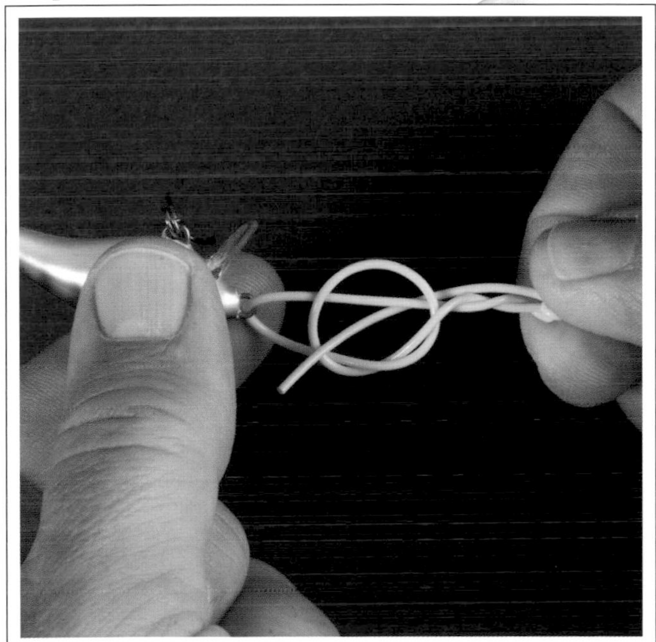

Take the working end through the overhand knot.

Rapala Knot: Step 4

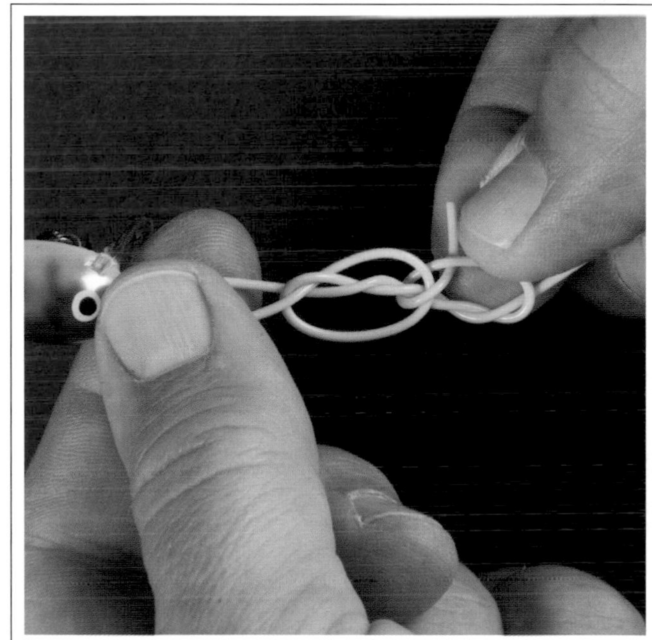

Take working end through the loop created in the standing part, as shown in the photograph, and tighten.

DROPPER LOOP

Creates a loop at a right angle to the main line.

Known to many as the blood loop (due to its similarity to the blood knot), the dropper loop creates a loop that sits at a right angle to the main line. To this loop fly fishermen attach an additional fly, known as a dropper. It could also be used to attach a sinker or an extra hook. To keep bait off the bottom, especially useful when fishing in surf, a heavy sinker is tied to the end of the line and the dropper loop used to attach a hook and bait that floats in the

Dropper Loop: Step 1

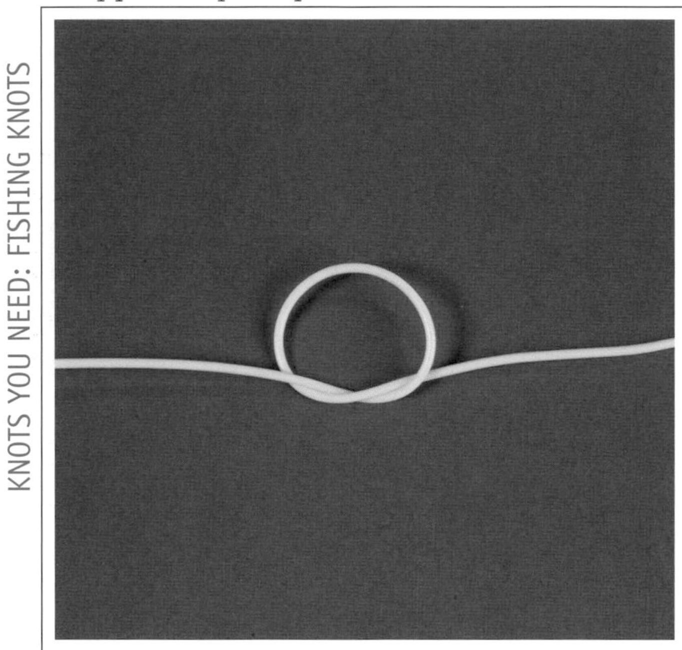

Tie an overhand knot (see page 18) in the line where the dropper loop will be needed.

Dropper Loop: Step 2

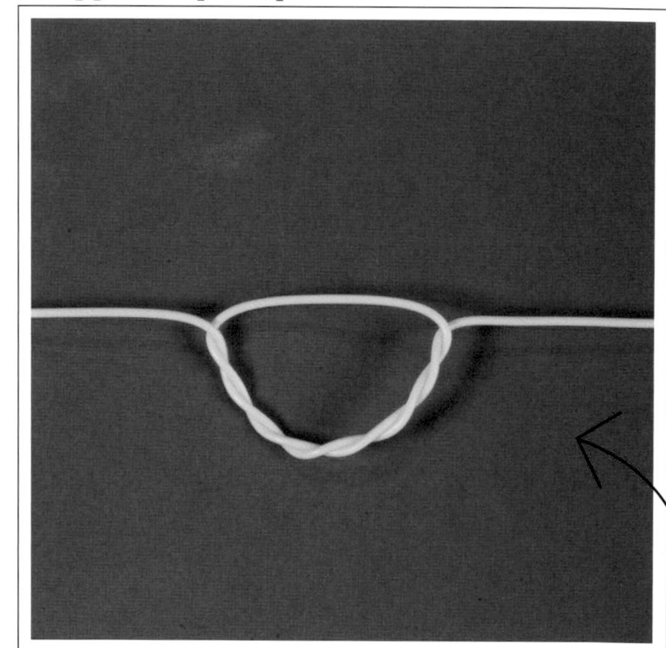

Bring the working end through the overhand several times to form a multiple overhand.

Have patience when working with these small knots. Tying knots of this size takes practice.

movement of the surf. This is a knot used only in fishing, and when tied correctly, the knot should look almost symmetrical on both sides of the loop.

Dropper Loop: Step 3

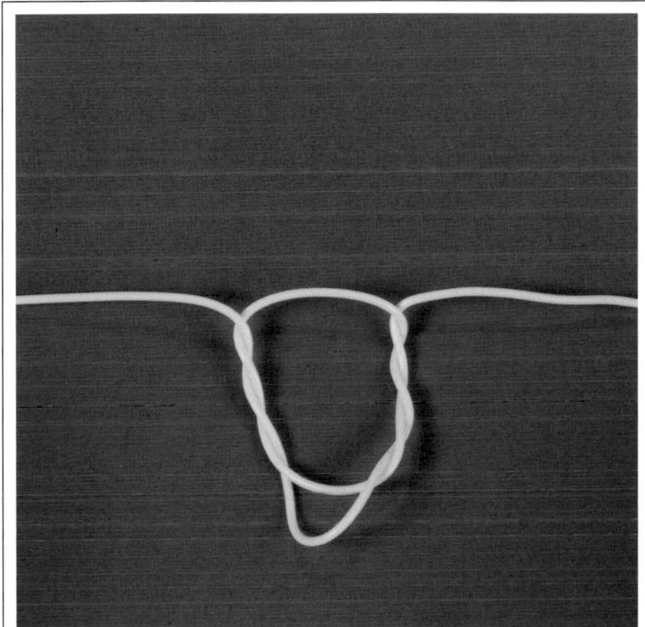

Create an opening in the middle of the multiple wraps of the overhand.

Dropper Loop: Step 4

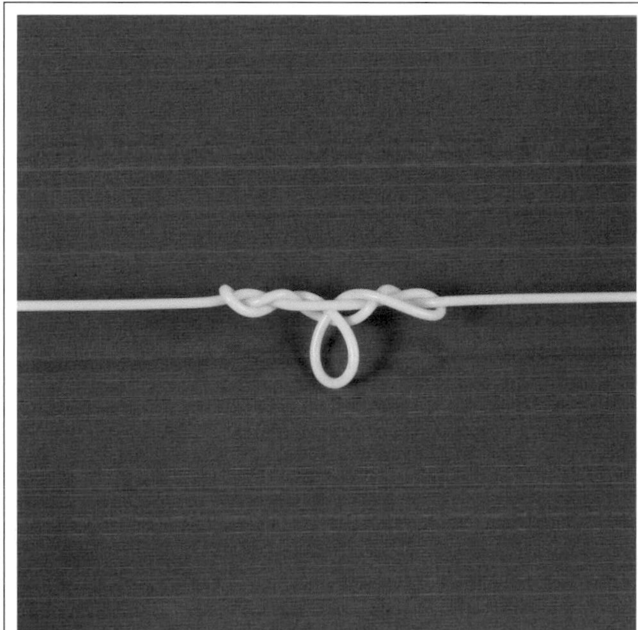

Pull the belly of the overhand, the middle of the part opposite the multiple wraps, down through the opening to create the dropper loop, and tighten by pulling on the standing parts.

DOUBLE OVERHAND LOOP

A simple and strong fixed loop for fishing line.

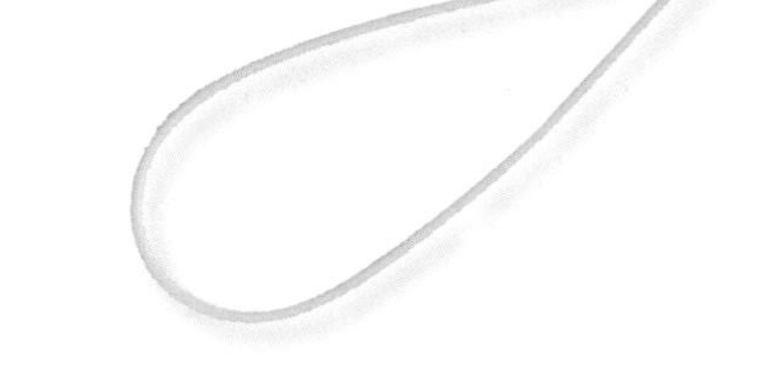

A double overhand knot (see page 52) tied on a bight creates a strong, fixed loop that works well in slick, modern material such as fishing line. Since it uses a bight, it can be tied at the end or anywhere else along a line. This knot jams in rope, but it can be used in twine or small cord.

Double Overhand Loop: Step 1

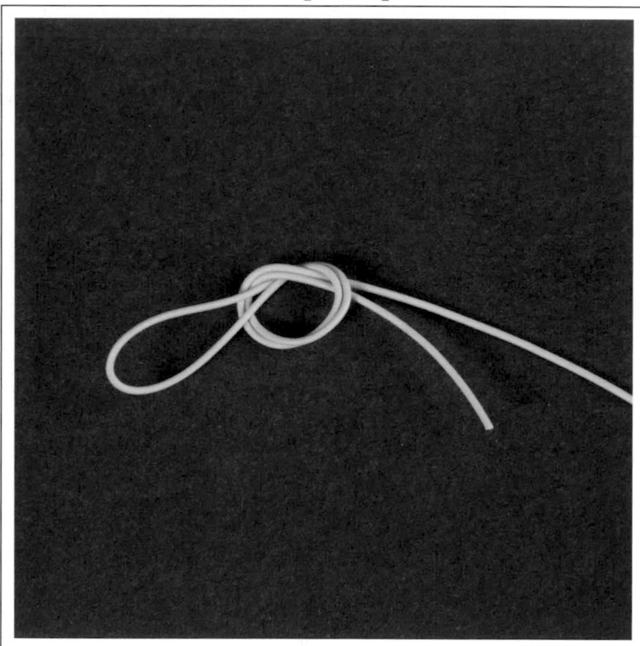

Form a bight in the line and tie an overhand knot (see page 18) in the bight.

GREEN ● LIGHT

This knot could be useful to campers.

Double Overhand Loop: Step 2

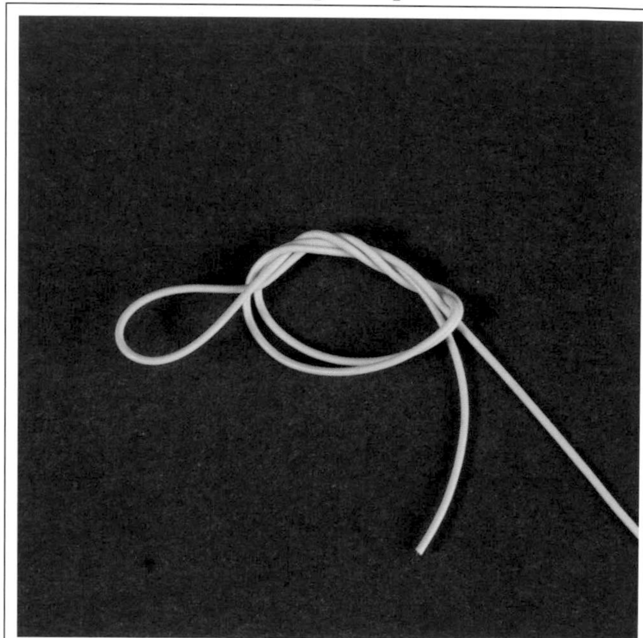

Tuck the bight through the overhand a second time to form a double overhand. Work slowly and carefully to form the final knot before full tightening.

JAPANESE BOWKNOT

Decorates the end of a cord.

The Japanese bowknot (sometimes simply called the Japanese knot) is tied at the end of a cord, making it a useful yet decorative addition to a pull-string. Once again, the knot work should be done on a flat surface for the most effective tying conditions. This knot is purely decorative.

Japanese Bowknot: Step 1

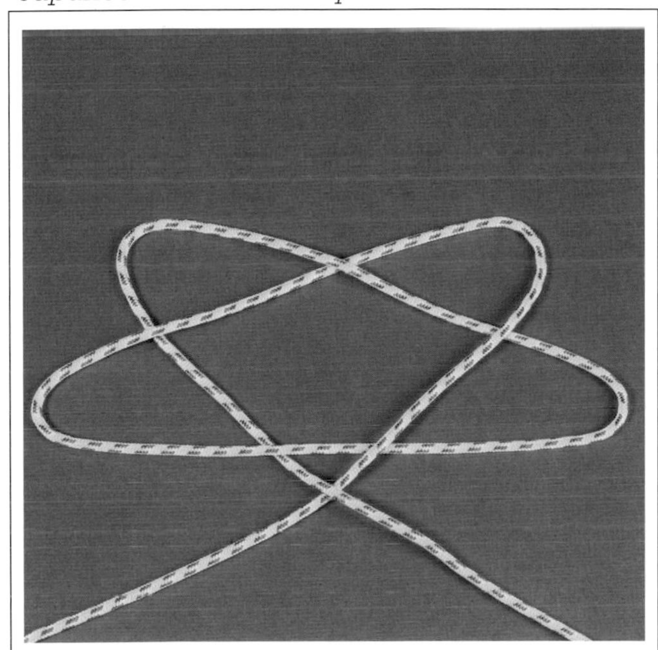

Lay out the cord as shown in the photograph.

The loops can be adjusted to the desired size during the final working.

Japanese Bowknot: Step 2

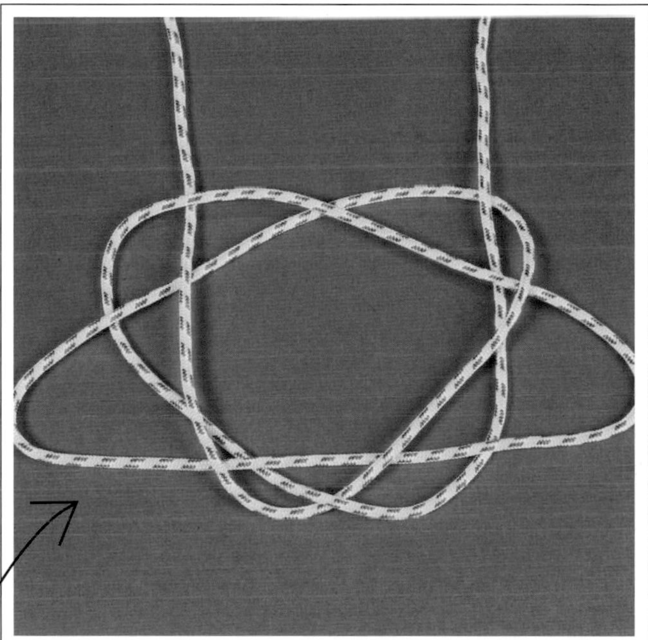

Bring the two ends up through the arrangement of cord as shown in the photograph. Work the knot, somewhat laboriously, into its final shape.

SIMPLE BOWKNOT

Ties two working ends quickly and easily together.

The simple bowknot (also known as the common bowknot or ordinary bowknot) is arguably the most used knot in the world. It is used to connect the ends of the laces of a pair of shoes, but it functions equally well any time two working ends need to be quickly and easily joined.

Despite its seemingly infinite usefulness, it is generally considered decorative (as all bowknots are) due to the pretty symmetry of the final form and the fact that it is used so often to decorate gifts. It unties even more easily than it ties; a tug on either working end will undo it.

Simple Bowknot: Step 1

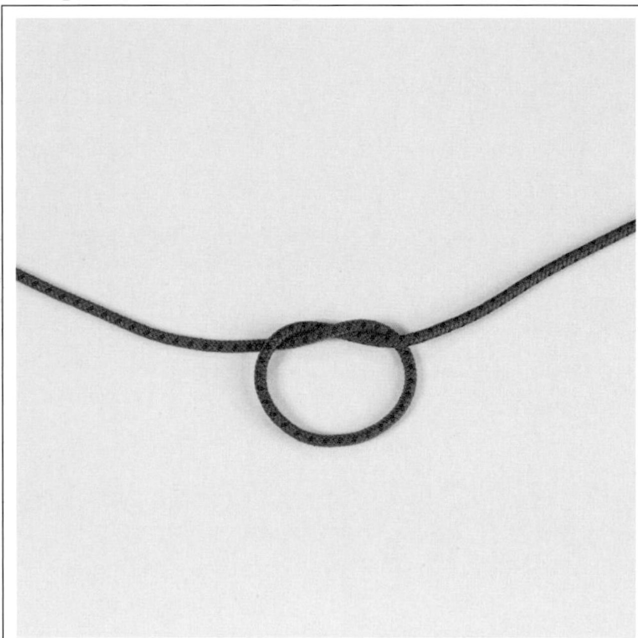

Tie the working ends together in an overhand knot (see page 18).

Simple Bowknot: Step 2

Form a bight in one working end.

GREEN LIGHT

This knot can be used for tying shoes and wrapping presents, among other things.

ZOOM

The simple bowknot is a modification of the square knot (or reef knot). It can also be tied as a modification of the granny knot. This illustration, therefore, shows the granny form.

Simple Bowknot: Step 3

Form a bight in the second working end and wrap it around the first bight, as shown in the photograph.

Simple Bowknot: Step 4

Tighten by pulling on the two loops and adjust the size of the bow to the needed size.

SHEEPSHANK BOWKNOT

A variation of the sheepshank that forms a lovely bow.

The sheepshank bowknot is no more than a tightening of the common sheepshank knot in a way that creates a bow instead of the standard sheepshank configuration (see page 88). When slack is left in twine or string during the wrapping of a package, either intentionally or unintentionally, this knot can be used to decoratively remove the slack. The sheepshank knot is one that even the most accomplished knot tyers often claim never to have really used, despite the fact that it works well. The sheepshank bowknot, on the other hand, is one you will surely tie in string at least now and then.

Sheepshank Bowknot: Step 1

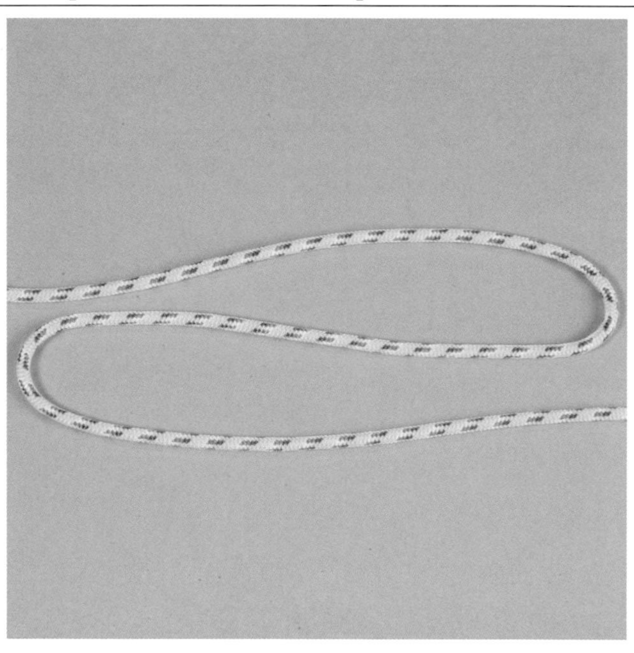

Lay out two bights in the cord in an *S* or *Z* shape.

Sheepshank Bowknot: Step 2

Use the main cord to tie two half hitches (see page 35) over the ends of both bights, as shown in the photograph.

ZOOM

The bow shape and an attractive symmetry of loops are the common characteristics of all the bowknots. Decorative knots are functional, too, and are used to highlight gifts.

Sheepshank Bowknot: Step 3

Pull on both of the main parts of the cord to take the slack out of the cord.

Sheepshank Bowknot: Step 4

Pull on both of the loops to create the bowknot shape, then tighten.

The sizes of the loops may be adjusted before final tightening.

TRUE LOVER'S KNOT

A multi-use entanglement for a bow or lanyard.

The legend goes something like this: In the sixteenth century, Dutch sailors began to intertwine two overhand knots to form a new knot they called the true lover's knot. The intertwined overhand knots represented intertwined lovers—the lovers, supposedly, they left behind. What is not legend is this: The name became very popular, and today quite a few knots bear the name *true lover's*. It is also factual that all true lover's knots share the intimate mating of two overhands knots into a symmetrical whole. Thus the fisherman's knot (see page 106) may

True Lover's Knot: Step 1

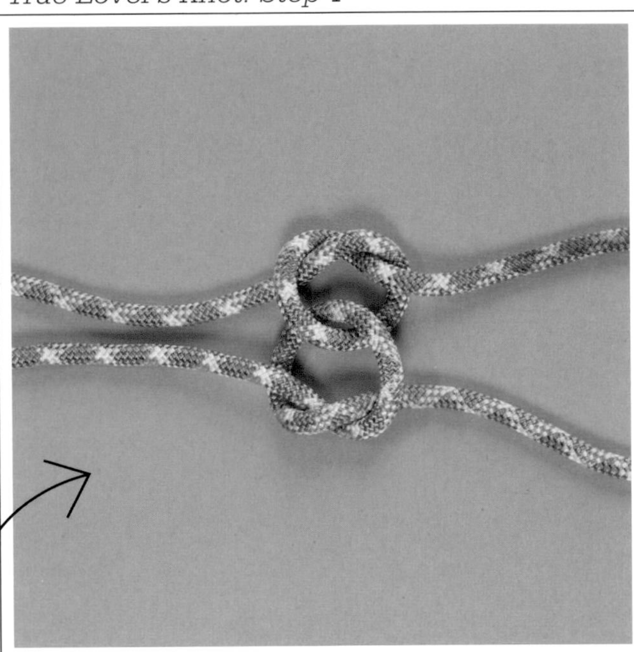

Intertwine two overhand knots (see page 18) on opposite sides of a bight, as shown in the photograph. The overhands must be intertwined exactly as shown.

At this point, the cord may be tightened into a lanyard knot.

True Lover's Knot: Step 2

Take the belly of one overhand out through the opposite overhand, as shown in the photograph.

occasionally be called a true lover's knot.

True lover's knots, when aggressively tightened, tend to be somewhat difficult to untie, another piece of symbolism for the romantically inclined. In addition to cordage, true lover's knots also appear often in jewelry.

BOWKNOTS

With patience, the size of the loops can be adjusted.

True Lover's Knot: Step 3

Take the belly of the second overhand out through the opposite overhand, as shown in the photograph.

True Lover's Knot: Step 4

Pull on both loops of the bow to tighten the knot.

SIMPLE LANYARD KNOT

Small ornamental embellishment or short piece of cord attached to an object.

Lanyards originally were—and still can be—short pieces of cord attached to any object to hold it, usually around the neck or wrist, or to act as a handle. Today lanyard knots are seen primarily as decorative. One of many single-strand lanyard knots, this simple one can be used to decorate thin cord that hangs otherwise unattractively. In thicker cord it fails to tighten into its attractive shape. It can be tied in a series along a cord to shorten the cord or to make the cord easier to grip. This knot could be useful to campers or boaters who want to shorten a piece of cord and/or make it easier to handle.

Simple Lanyard Knot: Step 1

Tie a figure 8 knot (see page 22) in the cord but do not tighten it.

Simple Lanyard Knot: Step 2

Bring each end of the cord through the opposite loop in the figure 8 and tighten.

FOUR-PLY KNOT

Small ornamental embellishment to an otherwise uninteresting length of cord.

Lanyard knots were born on sailing ships and sometimes used as stoppers. They all share the characteristic of the cord entering and leaving the knot on opposite ends. Many, such as the four-ply knot, can be used to separate beads on a necklace or add attractiveness to the pull-strings on lights, dog leashes, and window blind cords.

Four-Ply Knot: Step 1

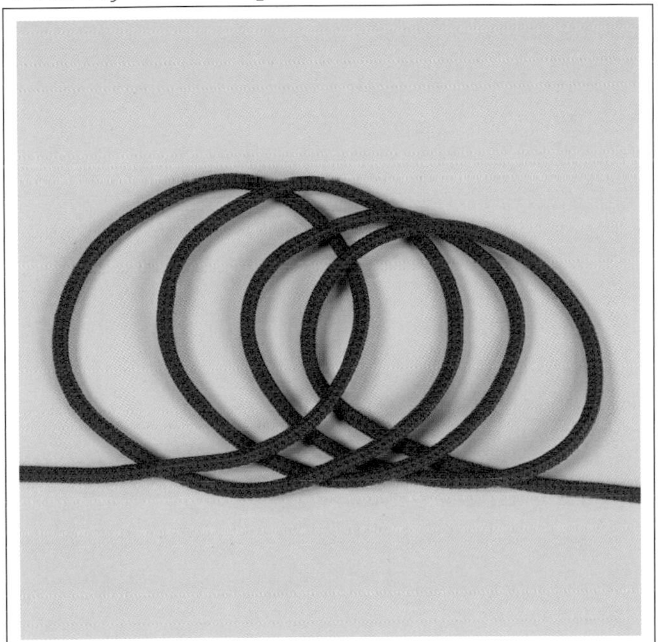

Lay out the cord in four interlaced loops as shown in the photograph.

Four-Ply Knot: Step 2

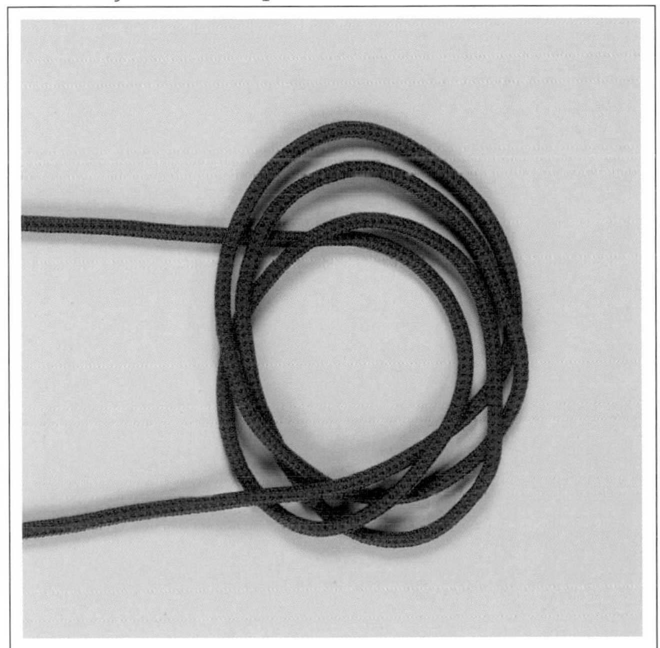

Bring the two ends down, as shown in the photograph, and meticulously work the slack out of the cord before tightening the knot.

FIVE-LEAD FLAT-SINNET

Intertwined strands that form a larger lanyard knot.

Sinnets all share the common characteristic of one or more intertwined strands and have many decorative applications. The five-lead flat-sinnet is another single-strand lanyard knot that creates a pretty entanglement of cord larger than the simple lanyard knot, or blimp knot, and the four-ply knot. It ties with relative ease and can be used to shorten a dangling cord with one knot instead of series of knots.

Sinnet originated as a maritime term for braided cord but today sees wider use as a term that refers to

Five-Lead Flat-Sinnet: Step 1

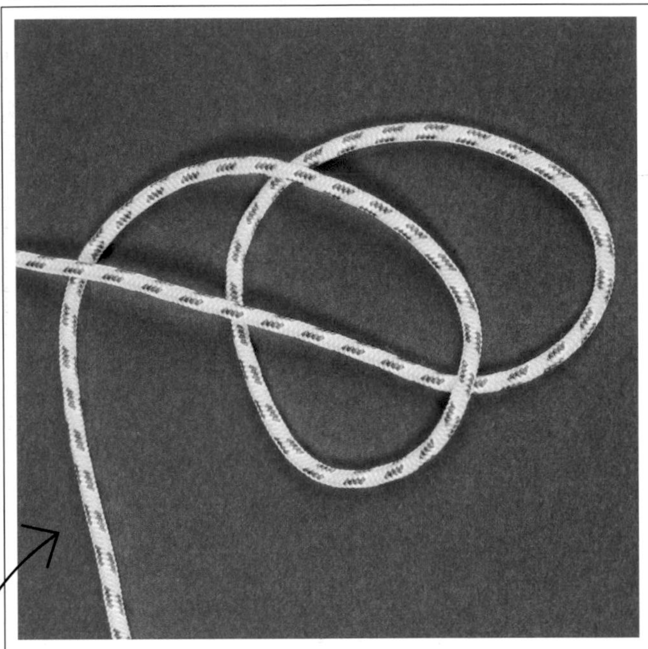

Arrange the cord as shown in the photograph.

Working on a flat surface will make this process easier.

Five-Lead Flat-Sinnet: Step 2

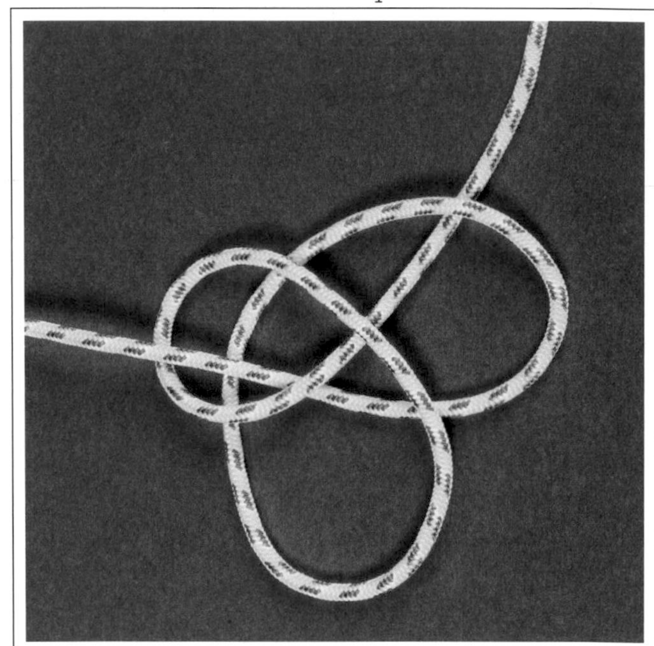

Begin to plait (or braid) the cord by twisting the outside left strand over into the center.

any braided cordage. It can be braided flat, round, or square. Generally speaking, there are three categories of sinnets: braided (or plaited) sinnets; chain sinnets; and crown sinnets, a series of crown knots tied on top of each other to form a long, squared shape. Decorative knot tying involves numerous variations within each of these categories.

Five-Lead Flat-Sinnet: Step 3

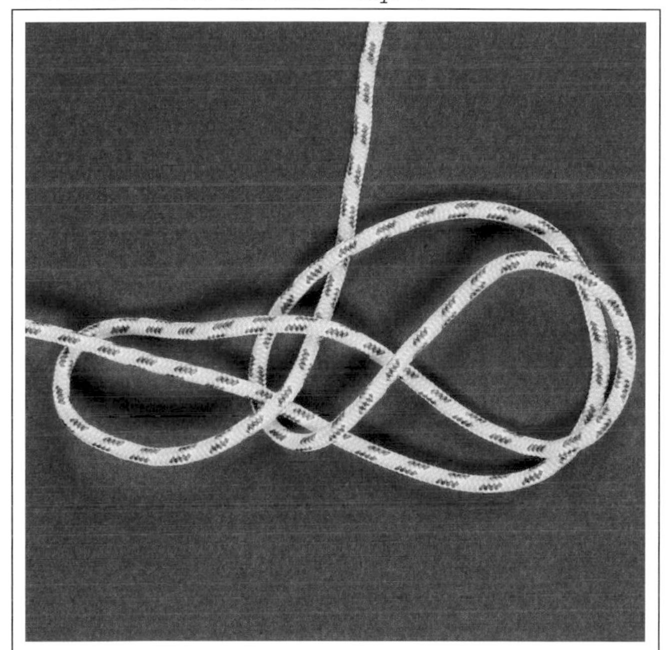

Continue to plait by bring the new outside left strand over into the center to form the arrangement in the photograph.

Five-Lead Flat-Sinnet: Step 4

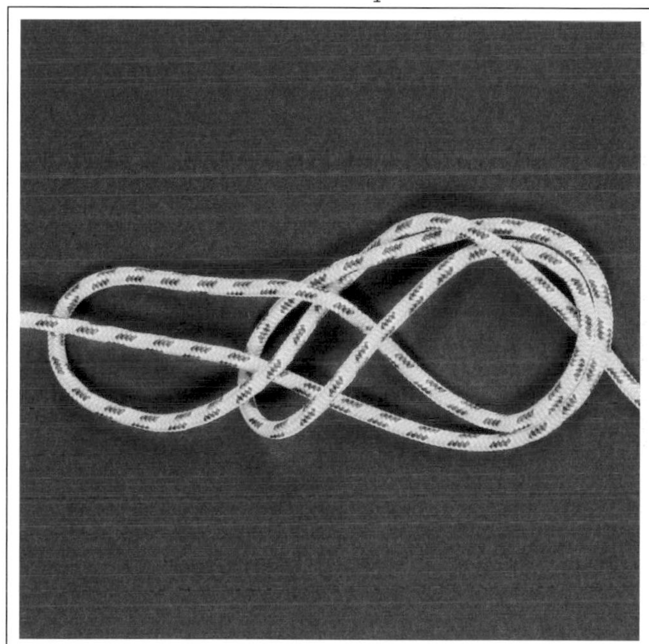

Tuck the outside right strand through the double loops, work out the slack, and slowly tighten the knot.

BRAID KNOT

Simple braiding of cord to form a much shorter cord.

When the cord (or lanyard) is too long, far too long, or even just a little too long, this simple braid knot in the cord will shorten it attractively to the required length. This knot works in just about any material—natural fiber cord, synthetic cord, thick or thin cord, leather, cloth, even human hair. Depending on the material, it may be seen almost anywhere from a waist tie on gowns to a prettily shortened window blind pull-string to a bright

Braid Knot: Step 1

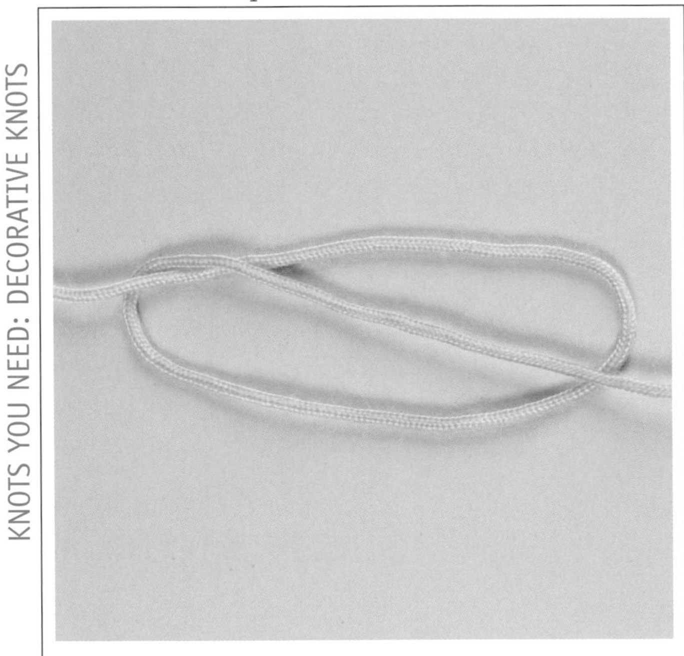

Arrange the cord in three parts as shown in the photograph.

Braid Knot: Step 2

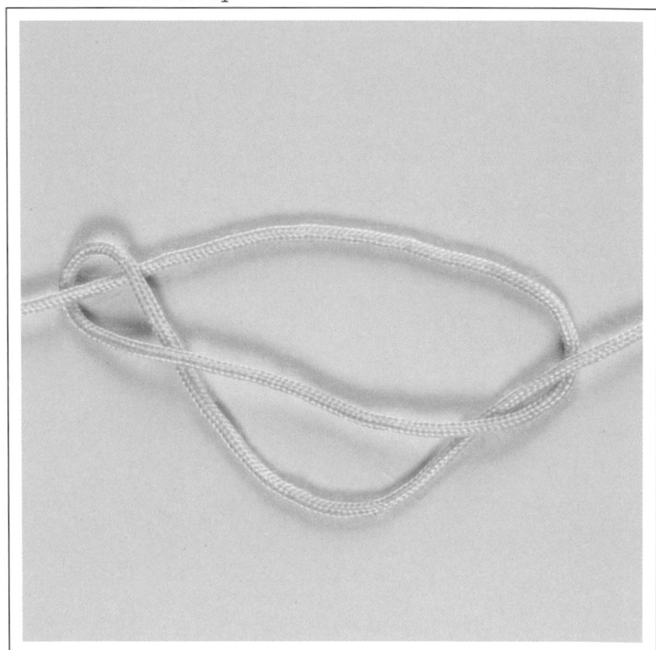

Bring the outside left strand to the center.

GREEN LIGHT

This knot can be used by campers and boaters, and by anyone else with a length of cord he or she wishes to shorten.

piece of perlon attached to a key ring. In sturdier material, it could be used to create a handle for a heavy package or improvise a broken handle for a suitcase.

The braid will keep tangling. To untangle, periodically pull out the free end of the cord

Braid Knot: Step 3

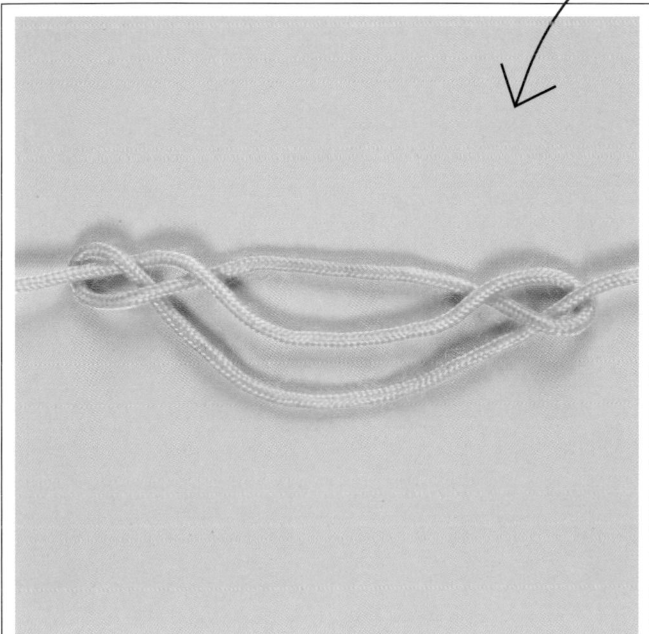

Bring the outside right strand to the center.

Braid Knot: Step 4

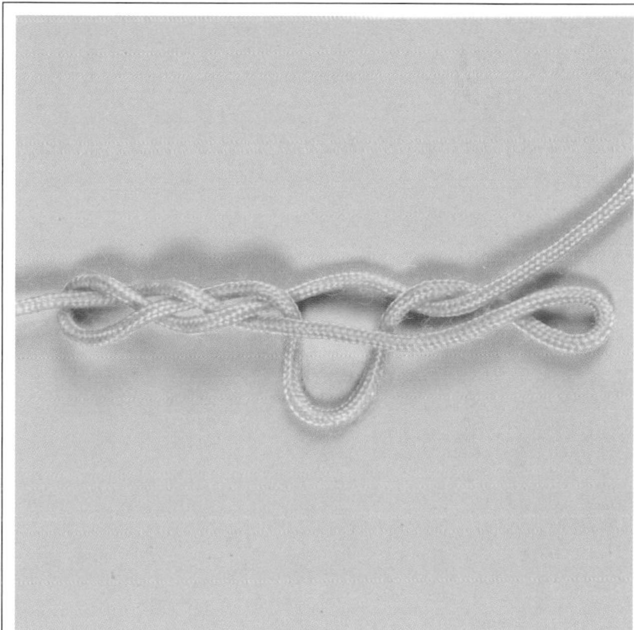

Continue braiding—left, then right—until the desired length is reached. Tuck the end through the final loop to lock the knot.

CROWN KNOT

Forms two single loops at right angles to the cord.

This crown knot is actually a modification of a true crown knot. It utilizes a single strand to create two single loops that sit at right angles to the center of the knot when the knot is drawn tight. As a lanyard knot, it can be used to decorate the lanyard or, more practically, to decoratively shorten the lanyard. (In this case, you adjust the size of the loops during tying to shorten the lanyard the desired amount.) It is sometimes tied around another cord or piece of twine to decorate a package.

This knot tends to slip apart if care is not taken to

Crown Knot: Step 1

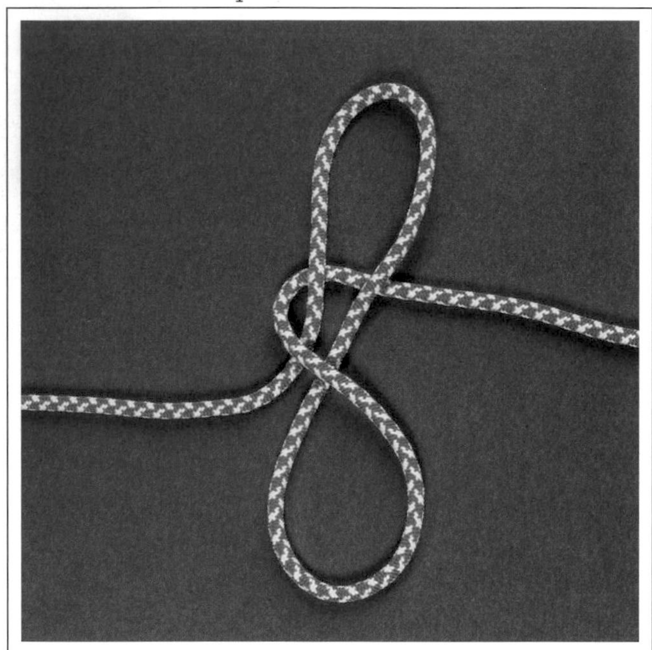

Arrange the cord as shown in the photograph.

Crown Knot: Step 2

Bring the end indicated in the photograph (that had previously been on the right side) back across the arrangement.

tighten it fully while forming the crown in the center. This is a finicky knot to tighten, but the result is worthy of your effort.

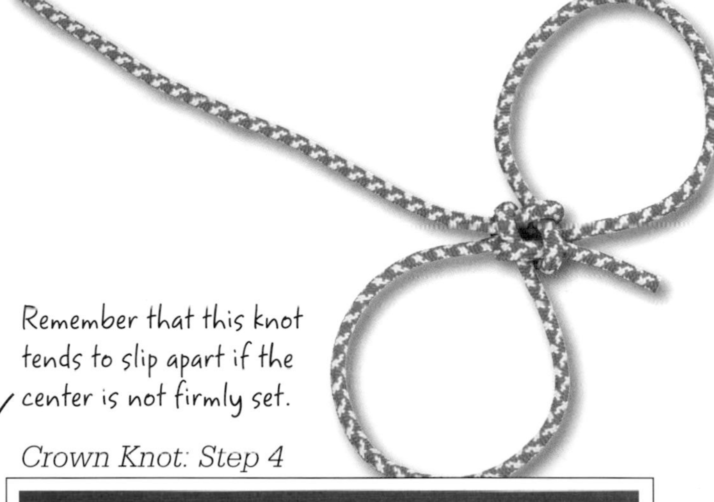

Remember that this knot tends to slip apart if the center is not firmly set.

Crown Knot: Step 3

Weave the end through the arrangement as shown in the photograph.

Crown Knot: Step 4

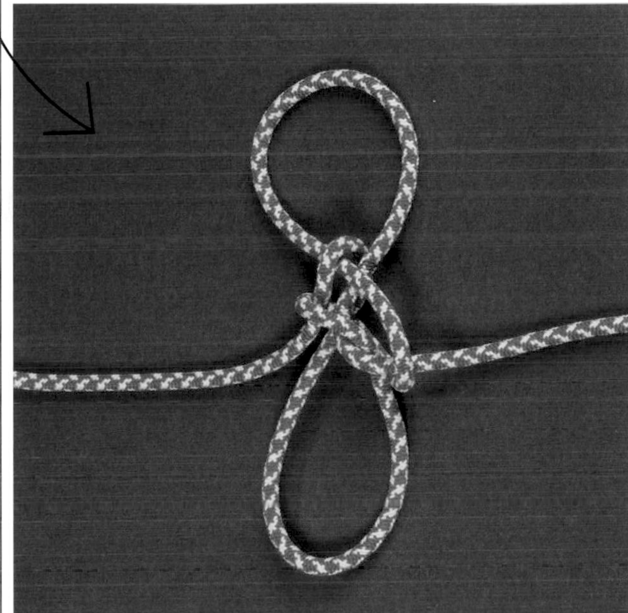

Work the knot slowly into its final form. You will need some patience, as this can be slightly time-consuming and tricky.

TWO-STRAND MATTHEW WALKER

A decorative knot that attaches two cords to each other.

The two-strand Matthew Walker is the simplest of lanyard knots involving two different cords. It can be used as a stopper or to decoratively end two parallel cords. It is also used as a divider between braids in more complex decorative knot work.

The tension in both cords must be matched exactly or else a space will be created between the two cords, ruining the symmetry.

Two-Strand Matthew Walker Knot: Step 1

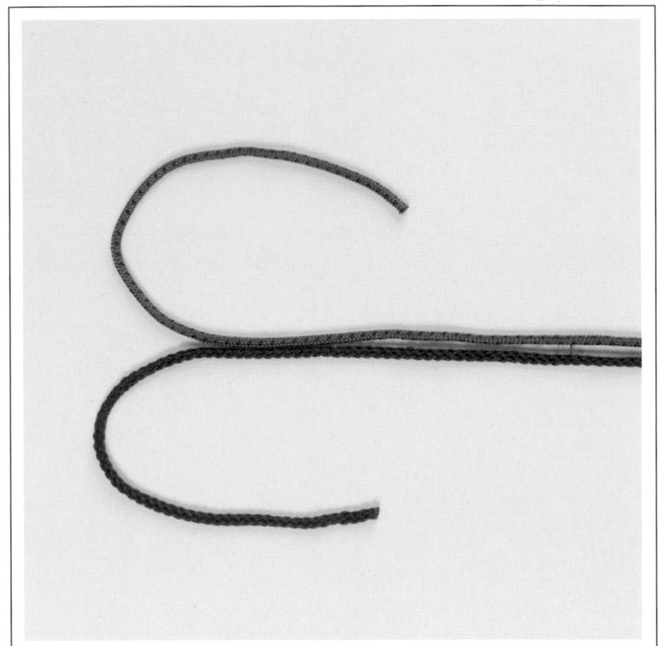

Hold the two cords parallel to each other with the ends forming two opposing bights, as shown in the photograph.

GREEN LIGHT

This knot can be used by campers and boaters.

Two-Strand Matthew Walker Knot: Step 2

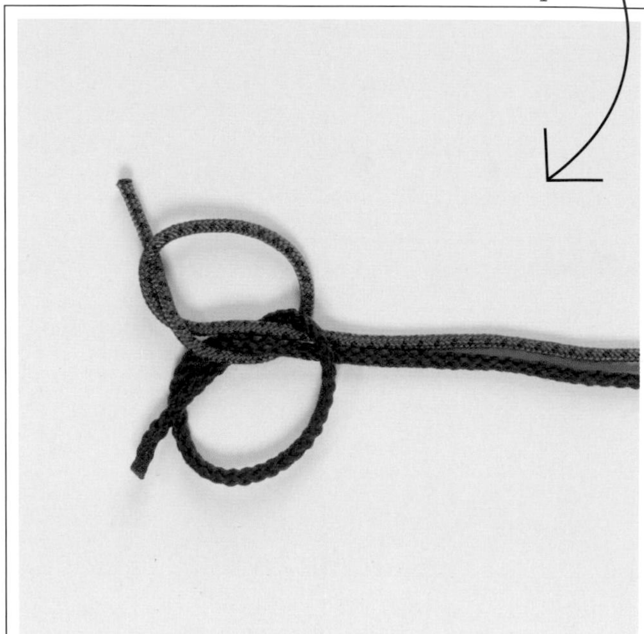

Take the working ends, one at a time, around both cords, through the opposite bight, and out the top of the bight to form two interlocked overhand knots (see page 18). Tighten slowly and carefully.

CHINESE BUTTERFLY KNOT

An intricate interweaving of two cords.

The term *Chinese butterfly* is used to describe a great number of knots, many of them highly ornate and elaborately complex. This one, in lanyard form, is on the small side, creating a neat curve at each of the four corners. The tying of this knot goes easier if the cords are laid on a flat surface and arranged appropriately before tightening.

Chinese Butterfly Knot: Step 1

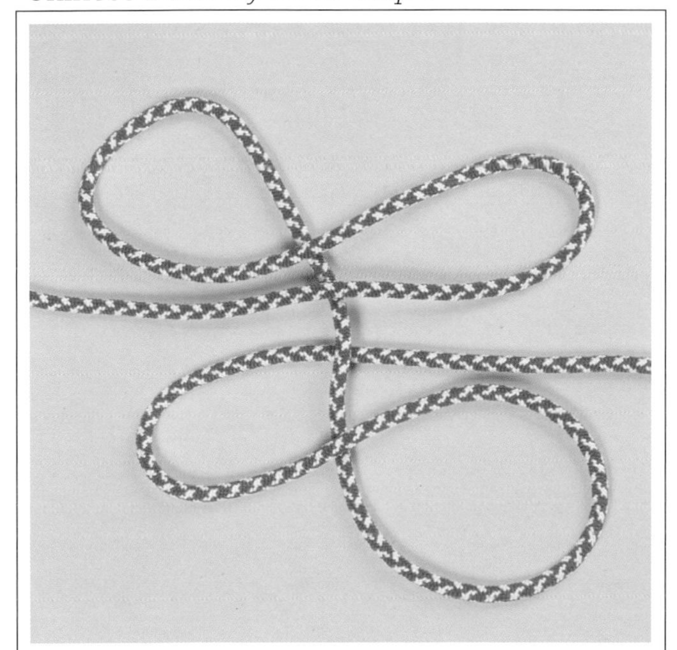

Arrange the first cord as shown above.

Chinese Butterfly Knot: Step 2

Painstakingly weave the second cord into the first cord as shown in the photograph. Slowly work the knot into its final and lovely form.

KNIFE LANYARD KNOT

This knot creates a fixed loop from which a knife—or another object—can be hung.

Considering its simplicity, this is certainly one of the most attractive lanyard knots—and, for that reason, one of the most often used. This knot was originally intended to create a fixed loop on a neck lanyard from which a seaman would suspend his knife. It can, of course, suspend many things and is known by other names, including the bosun's or boatswain's whistle knot, the pipe lanyard knot, and the two-strand diamond knot.

The loop behind your hand will be the final loop.

Knife Lanyard Knot: Step 1

Drape the cord over your left hand as shown in the photograph. Make a loop in the end of the cord (as shown) and hold the loop between your thumb and index finger (as shown).

Knife Lanyard Knot: Step 2

Bring the end indicated in the photograph (the end hanging down to the left side in the step 1 photo) up through the loop in your palm as shown in the photograph.

Depending on the object to be hung from the lanyard, sometimes the item must be strung onto the cord prior to the tying of the knot. Sometimes the object can be tied to the fixed loop by way of a girth (or ring) hitch (see page 98). Enthusiasts will notice that this knot is a relative of the carrick bend. Though it appears complex to tie, it's really not that difficult; just have patience tightening the knot.

Knife Lanyard Knot: Step 3

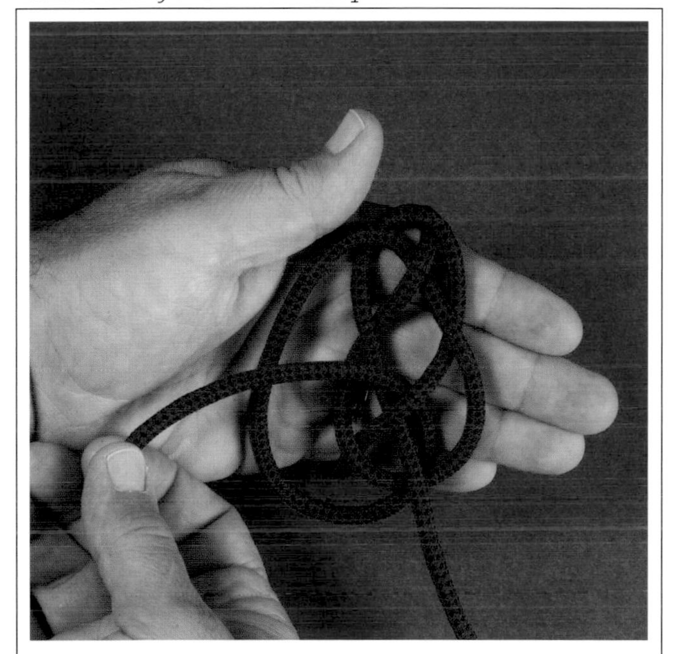

Bring the same end through the knot again as shown in the photograph.

Knife Lanyard Knot: Step 4

Bring the other end through the knot as shown in the photograph. Slip the arrangement off your hand and meticulously work the knot into its final form.

CHINESE BUTTON KNOT

A knot used to fasten garments decoratively.

Round, soft, and often highly decorative, button knots, as the name implies, are used to hold or fasten clothing together. In addition to being decorative, they are also highly durable—they don't break like plastic. Many popular button knots come from China, where traditional dresses and jackets still utilize them. Sometimes called pajama knots, they are mostly still used today in clothes worn for sleeping, in all parts of the world. They are also seen as decorative additions to other clothing, both fashionable and highly functional.

Chinese Button Knot: Step 1

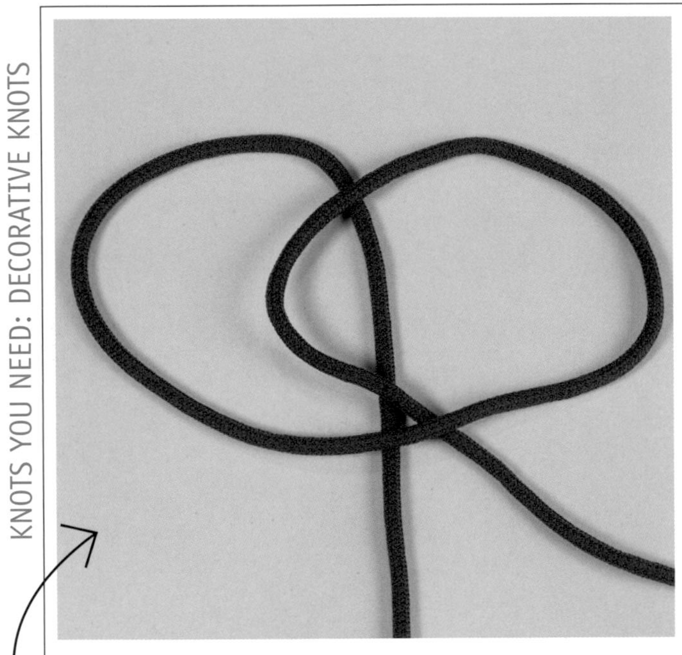

Begin by laying out two loops of cord as shown in the photograph.

Working on a flat surface will make this process easier.

Chinese Button Knot: Step 2

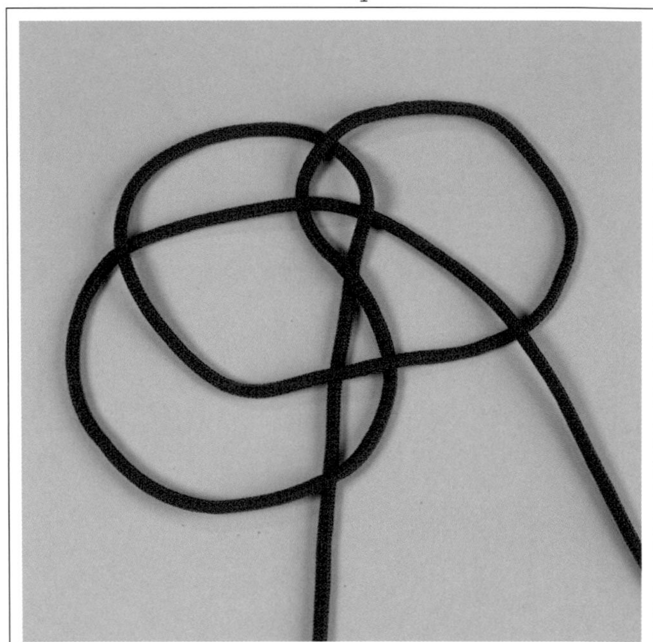

Add a third loop as shown in the photograph.

A button knot can be used to add interest to other cords, such as one used as a key chain. Sometimes, as you might imagine, knot enthusiasts tie them just because they're fun. The traditional Chinese button knot, the one shown here, with a complex interweaving of cord, may take some practice to achieve. Begin on a flat surface for easier tying

To fully tighten the knot, you may need to use needle-nose pliers (or tweezers for thin material).

Chinese Button Knot: Step 3

Continue to weave the end into the arrangement as shown, finishing with the two ends dropping down as shown to form the stem.

Chinese Button Knot: Step 4

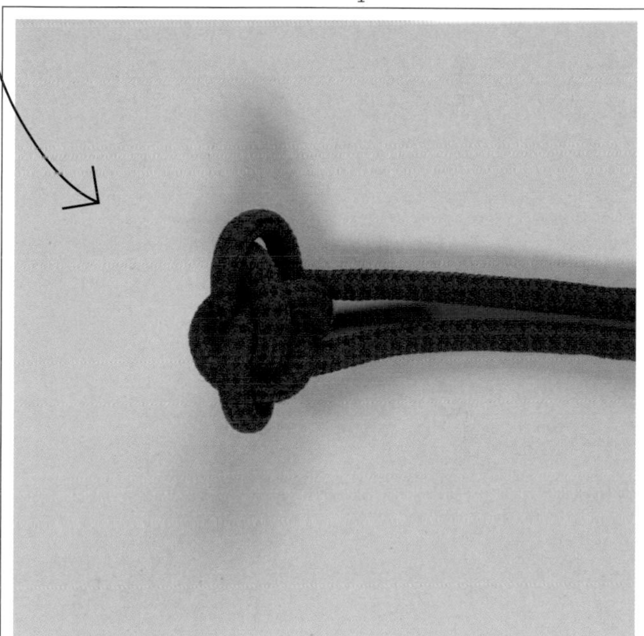

Slowly work out the surplus cord, drawing the knot up into a mushroom shape. Then carefully draw the knot up tightly into its final round shape.

EIGHT-PART BUTTON KNOT

A variation of the Chinese button knot.

This variation on the basic button knot alters a tuck in the knot to create a button that reveals eight surface parts. The traditional Chinese button knot (see page 184) has nine. As with all button knots, the working end and the standing part enter and leave the knot side by side.

Button knots appeared a time long before plastic buttons and were often preferred, because of their softness, to bone buttons. Due to the fragile nature of the material knots were tied in, little evidence of button knots remains for archaeologists to study, but button knots are revealed

Eight-Part Button Knot: Step 1

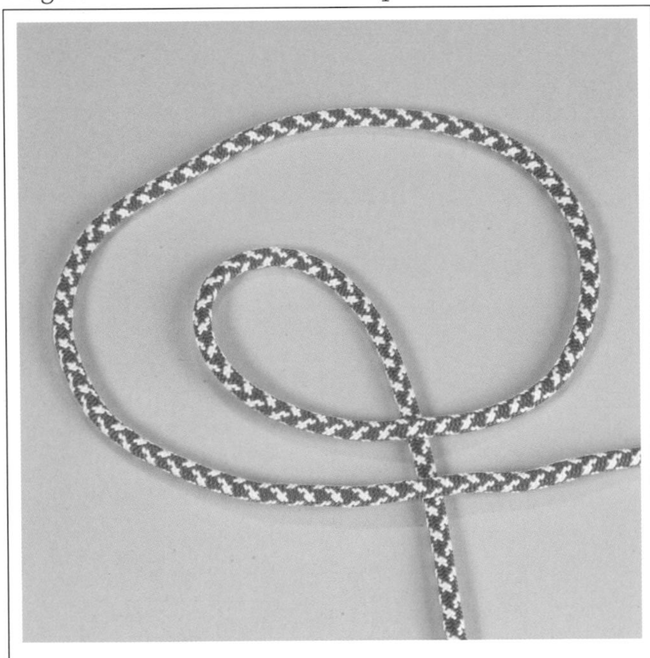

Begin by laying out the cord as shown in the photograph.

Eight-Part Button Knot: Step 2

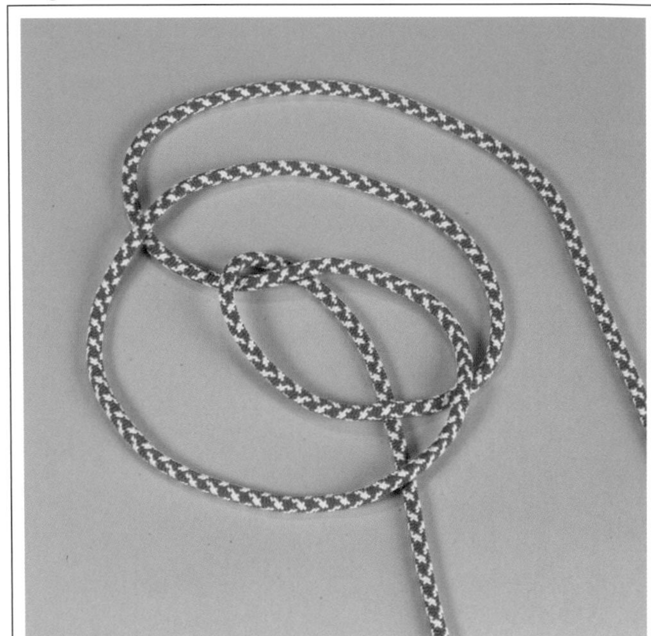

Continue to lay out and interweave the cord as shown in the photograph.

GREEN LIGHT

This knot can be used in garment making.

in Chinese art dating back approximately 2,500 years.

Once completed, the dangling cords of button knots are sewn to garments. If the buttonholes are too small for the knots, the cords are sewn with a loop left free. The loop is pushed through the buttonhole and then the button knot is pushed through the loop.

To fully tighten the knot, you may want to use needle-nose pliers (or tweezers for thin material).

Eight-Part Button Knot: Step 3

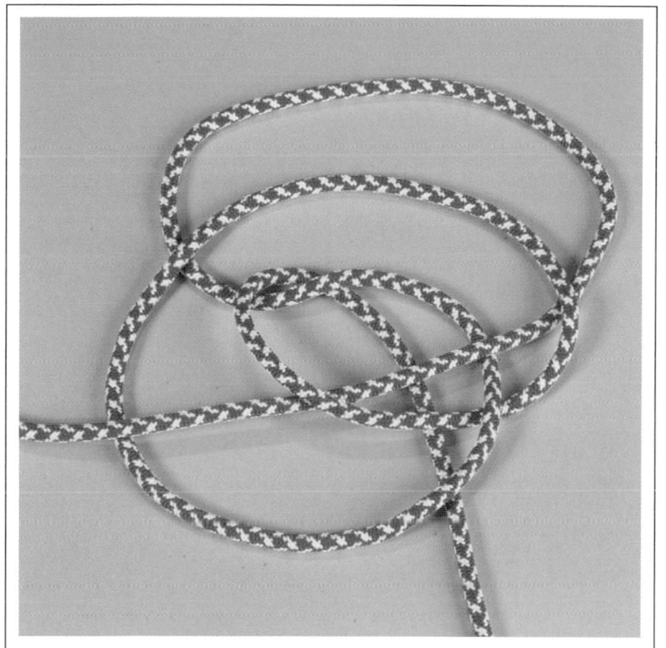

Continue to lay out and interweave the cord as shown in the photograph.

Eight-Part Button Knot: Step 4

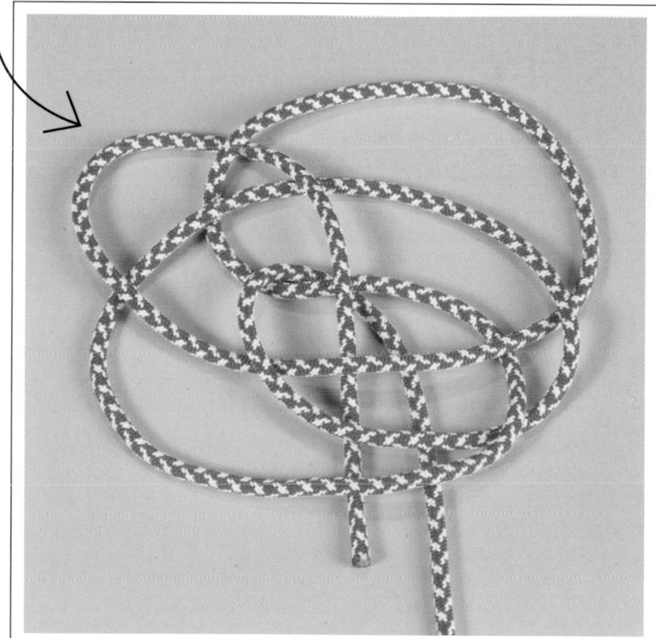

Add the final interweaving of the cord as shown, finishing with the two ends together in a stem. Slowly work out the surplus cord, working on a flat surface to begin, and draw the knot up into a mushroom shape. Then draw the knot up tightly into its final round shape.

MONKEY'S FIST

A large, round decorative knot with practical uses.

If you are imaginative, the monkey's fist (monkey fist, monkey paw) does resemble a fist. It may well be the most famous decorative knot, one recognized almost instantly by a vast number of people. It was probably developed by sailors who needed a heavy heaving line knot and who sometimes tied it around a stone or other spherical object to add weight. The knot can be tied around a rubber ball if flotation is desired.

Decoratively, the monkey's fist is popular as a large and attractive end to any cord, especially if the cord will

Monkey's Fist: Step 1

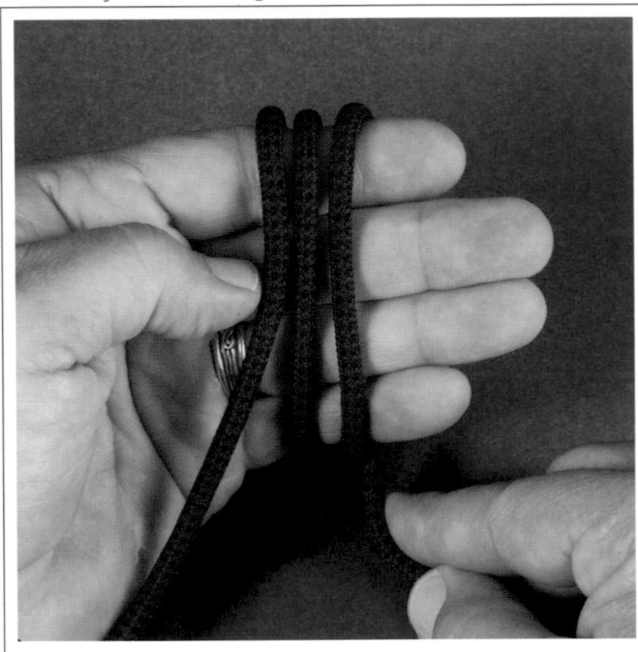

Wrap the cord around your hand as shown in the photograph.

Monkey's Fist: Step 2

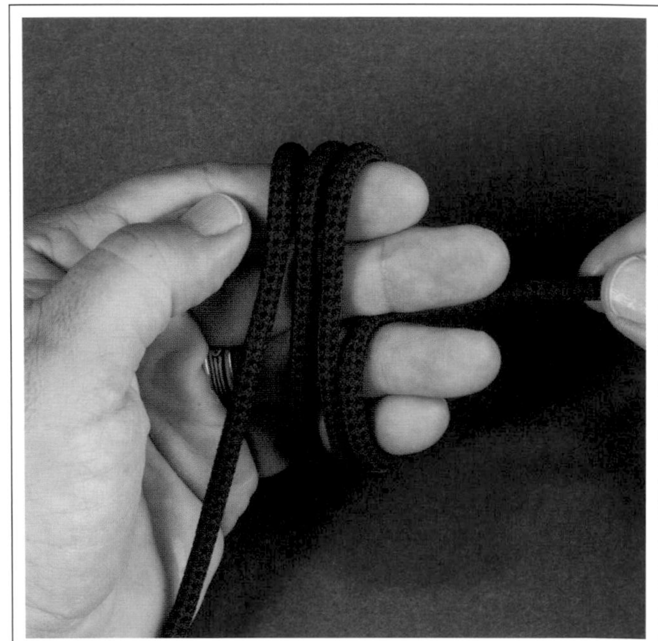

Trap the final wrap with your fingers as shown.

be used as a pull-string. It is most often tied as a two-ply or three-ply knot. (A three-ply knot is illustrated here). It can be tied larger than a three-ply. In addition to being tied around a spherical object (a marble or golf ball would work fine for decorative purposes), it can be tied around your hand as a starting point; this is known as the sailor's method and is shown here.

Monkey's Fist: Step 3

Slip the upper half of the wraps off your fingers and continue to wrap an equal number of wraps around the first set of wraps, as shown in the photograph. A spherical object may be inserted at this point.

Be sure to tuck the end inside the knot to hide it.

Monkey's Fist: Step 4

With the bundle entirely off your fingers, make a third set of wraps, the same in number, around and through where the two bundles of cord meet. It will take some time to tighten and form the ball into its final spherical shape.

TURK'S HEAD

A decorative embellishment to cylindrical or semi-cylindrical objects.

The Turk's head, often spoken of as the ultimate decorative knot, actually has many applications that include functioning as a napkin ring, providing better grip to a railing, and marking the center rudder position of a ship's wheel. Variations are virtually without number, all called Turk's heads, and all based on the length of cord available and the ability (and patience) of the tyer. Some enthusiasts have devoted themselves entirely to this knot, writing books about it.

Yes, it does sort of resemble a turban, and thus the

Turk's Head: Step 1

Wrap the cord around your hand as shown in the photograph, making sure to leave a long length of cord to work with.

Turk's Head: Step 2

Carefully slip the loops off your hand and tuck the right-hand loop through the left-hand loop.

name. Never the exclusive result of a sailor's skill, both South American and western U.S. cowboys tied very complex Turk's heads.

Be sure to tuck the ends inside the knot to hide them.

Turk's Head: Step 3

Bring the working end down through the knot as shown in the photograph.

Turk's Head: Step 4

Slip the arrangement carefully over the object through the loops created. Weave the working end over and under the object, through the knot following the lead of the cord and always keeping the working end on the same side of the lead. The lead can be followed as many times as you wish.

SIMPLE CHAIN SINNET

Successive loops tucked neatly through each other to form a chain.

Chain sinnets, of which there are quite a few, have in common one or more strands that are formed into loops successively tucked into each other. A chain sinnet could be used to shorten a cord, as lanyard knots sometimes are, but this simple chain sinnet also creates the decorative gold braid seen on military uniform caps and shoulders. It is sometimes known as the trumpet cord since it decorates the gold cord often dangling from military trumpets (or, more accurately, military bugles). It may also be called the monkey chain or the monkey braid.

Simple Chain Sinnet (Monkey Chain): Step 1

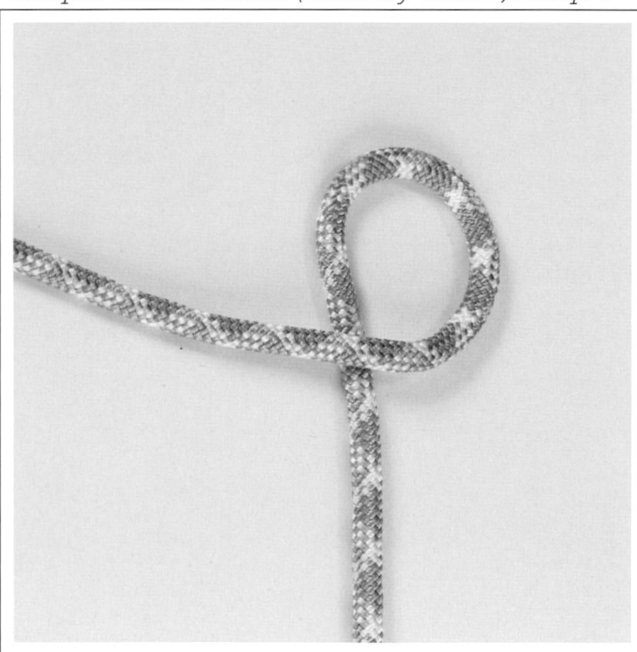

Form a loop in the cord.

GREEN LIGHT

This knot is also used by campers and climbers who need to store short pieces of cord or rope.

Simple Chain Sinnet (Monkey Chain): Step 2

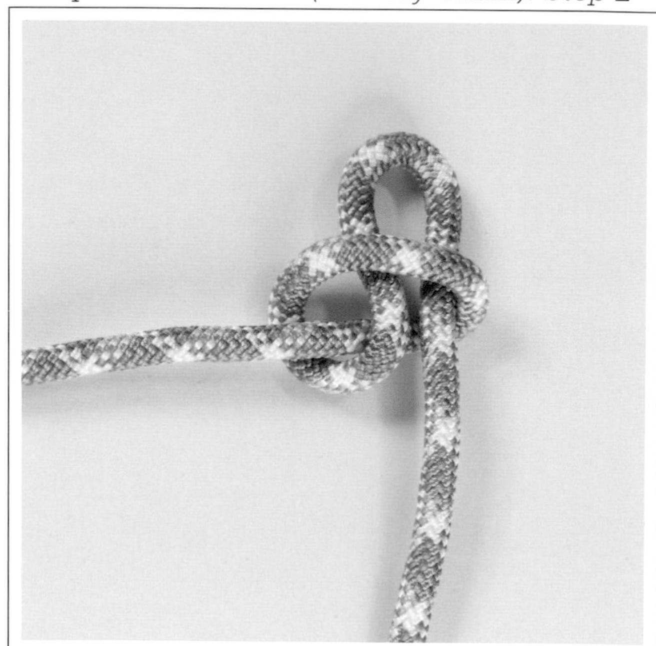

Tuck a second loop of the cord through the first loop as shown in the photograph. An overhand with draw loop has now been tied in the cord.

The simple chain sinnet is the chain sinnet most often used in the world of knot tying. In addition to being decorative, it also serves, when tied loosely, as a method of packing short pieces of cord or rope in a manner that prevents tangling. This method allows the cord or rope to be untied from the chain with ease. Once tied, the cord assumes an interesting elasticity.

No tightening is necessary if the cord or rope is being prepared for packing or storage.

Simple Chain Sinnet (Monkey Chain): Step 3

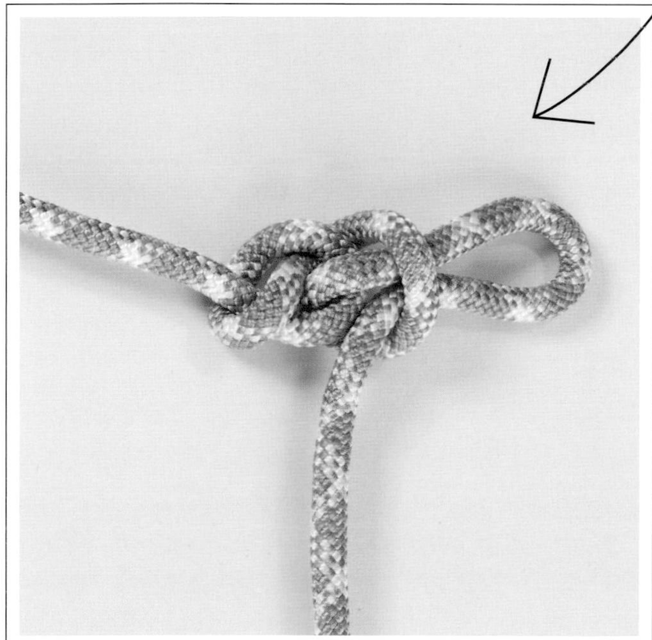

Tuck a third loop through the second loop. At this point begin to tighten and arrange the loops as you go along.

Simple Chain Sinnet (Monkey Chain): Step 4

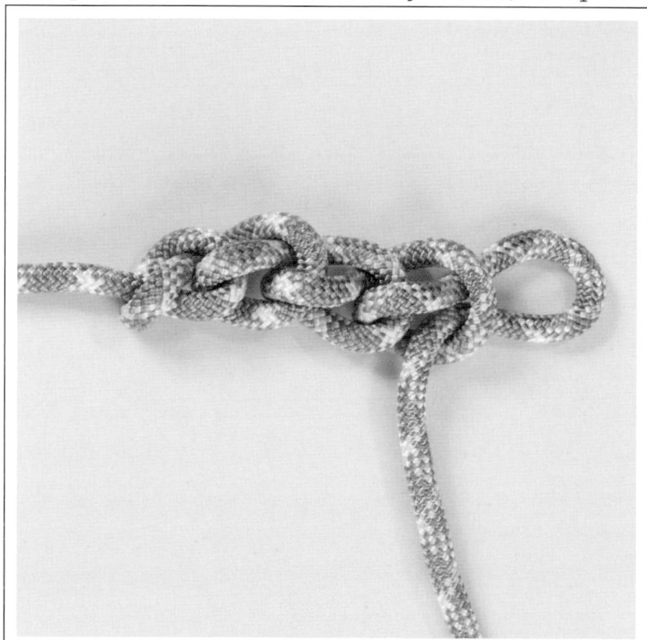

Continue to add loops to the sinnet until you reach the desired length. Thread the working end through the final loop to lock the knot.

CHINESE FLAT KNOT

A knot that lies flat to form a mat.

Flat knots, as the name suggests, lie flat and are essentially, though not technically, two-dimensional knots. There are many flat knots, most commonly used as mats for the home or boat. They may function as trivets for the table or to decoratively protect areas from rubbing such as where potted plants rest on furniture. The Chinese flat knot enlarges a carrick bend (see page 54), joining two cords of the same diameter. The cords may be the same color or contrasting colors—but with contrasting colors the interweaving is easier to follow, at least for someone

Chinese Flat Knot: Step 1

Lay the cord as if beginning a carrick bend (see page 54) as shown in the photograph.

Chinese Flat Knot: Step 2

Begin to tuck the four diagonal ends back through the bend as shown in the photograph.

new to flat knots. The Chinese flat knot is not especially difficult to tie, but it may take a few tries before the novice can tie it with ease.

The term "Chinese knot" also refers to the entire art of tying knots for decorative purposes in China, to many people representing the pinnacle of decorative knot tying.

Chinese Flat Knot: Step 3

Continue to weave the ends back over and under through the expanding knot as shown.

The ends can be tied off in decorative knots as a final touch, with knots such as double overhands.

Chinese Flat Knot: Step 4

Weave the diagonal ends through the knot until you reach the desired size. Size is determined by the will of the tyer and/or the length of the cords. Arrange the knot into its final form, which is not tight but with spaces between the interwoven strands of the knot.

KNOTS IN ACTION

Climbing Knot: Figure 8 with follow through with double overhand

PHOTO BY KATE CALDER, CLIMBER IS MARK CALDER

PHOTO BY STEPHANIE YOUNG MERZEL

Fishing Knot: Tying Fishing Knot

Boat Knot: Square (Reef) Knot

PHOTO BY JESSICA KEOGH

Climbing Knot: Munter-Mule hitch with Figure 8 backup

PHOTO BY DWAYNE CAMPOGAN

Camping/Boating Knot: Clove hitch tied in a bight

PHOTO BY ANDY PIXEL

PHOTO BY MICHAEL HORNUNG

Decorative Knot: Turk's Head

Camping/Climbing Knot: Prusik, Blake Hitch, Double Figure 8, Figure 8

PHOTO BY JOHN MONTGOMERY

Climbing Knot: Firth Hitch, Prusik knot

PHOTO BY DWAYNE CAMPOGAN

PHOTO BY MICHAEL HORNUNG

Decorative Knot: Simple Lanyard Knot (4 lead diamond knot)

Boating Knot: Overhand Knot.

PHOTO BY TROY B. THOMAS

PHOTO BY MICHAEL HORNUNG

Decorative Knot: Turk's Head

PHOTO BY TROY B. THOMAS

Camping Knot: Loops made with double over-hand knots.

Versatile Knot: Overhand Knot being used as a stopper.

PHOTO BY TROY B. THOMAS

PHOTO BY JACKK

Camping Knot: Clove Hitch on a stake backed up with an Overhand Draw Loop.

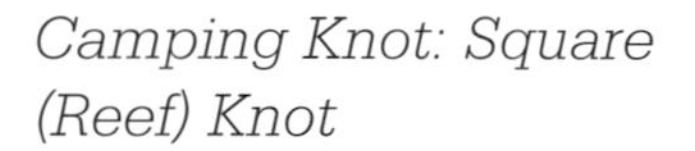

Camping Knot: Square (Reef) Knot

PHOTO BY RADHOOSE

PHOTO BY SHARKY

Camping Knot: Clove Hitch

Climbing Knot: Girth Hitch

PHOTO BY GRAEME DAWES

INDEX